SELECTED POEMS OF
Gabriela Mistral

SELECTED POEMS OF

Gabriela Mistral

TRANSLATED AND EDITED BY

DORIS DANA

WOODCUTS BY ANTONIO FRASCONI

PUBLISHED FOR THE LIBRARY OF CONGRESS
BY THE JOHNS HOPKINS PRESS / BALTIMORE

1. Latin American Poetry

The Johns Hopkins Press, Baltimore, Maryland 21218
The Johns Hopkins Press Ltd., London

Library of Congress Catalog Card Number 77-137467
ISBN 0-8018-1197-X (clothbound edition)
ISBN 0-8010-1256-9 (paperback edition)

HISPANIC FOUNDATION PUBLICATIONS

A series issued under a co-operative agreement between The Johns Hopkins
University and the Library of Congress to include works prepared and published
on private funds, especially those furnished to the Library by the Ford Foundation
for expansion of Hispanic Foundation activities.

This book is dedicated to Gabriela herself,
with great love.

Among the many thousands of pages of manuscript
she left behind, I came upon one small fragment
that says: *They shall not die. No, no one dies
except he who has never lived.*

Contents

Foreword by Francisco Aguilera

Gabriela Mistral occupies a unique place in literary history as the first Latin American writer to be awarded the Nobel Prize for Literature. This distinction was conferred upon her in Stockholm on November 15, 1945. The international recognition of her poetic genius was a source of special rejoicing not only in her native Chile but throughout Latin America. To this day, she and the Guatemalan novelist Miguel Angel Asturias, who was given the Nobel Prize in 1967, are the only two Latin Americans to have received the award.

In 1914, nearly thirty-one years before Gabriela Mistral won the Nobel Prize, she participated in a national poetry contest without precedent in the austere milieu of Chilean literary life. Under the pseudonym of Gabriela Mistral she submitted a trio of sonnets entitled "*Los Sonetos de la Muerte*" ("Sonnets of Death"). She was then a young unknown schoolteacher, Lucila Godoy Alcayaga, living in a northern provincial town where she had, from the age of fifteen, been contributing poems to local papers under a variety of pen names. Some of her works had already been published in a Paris fashion magazine, *Elegancias*, whose editor was none other than Rubén Darío. It was in his magazine that she used for the first time the pseudonym Gabriela Mistral, a name derived from the Archangel Gabriel and the fierce mistral wind that blows over the south of France. With her "Sonnets of Death," Gabriela won the Chilean national prize for poetry. One of Chile's leading literary critics, Hernán Díaz Arrieta, has said of them: "They are the most intense poems of love and sorrow in the Spanish language." These three poems, along with some fifty poems and stories published in 1917, established her as an important national writer.

The Chilean Ministry of Education began to take notice of Gabriela, and between 1918 and 1922 it forwarded her teaching career by waiving the requirement of pedagogic diplomas and appointing her to the rank of principal in *liceos*, first in Punta Arenas, Chile's southernmost city; then in Temuco, a refuge of the ancient Araucanian Indian; and finally in the capital, Santiago. Word of her spread abroad, through France and Spain, as well as through Latin America. In 1922 the Mexican Minister of Education, José Vasconcelos, officially invited Gabriela to come to his country to collaborate with him in carrying out an ambitious program of educational reform, including the teaching of Indian adults and children in isolated rural areas. It was in Mexico City that a school was first named after this young teacher, and a statue of her was erected in her honor in the courtyard. Today there is no country in Latin America that does not have several schools bearing her name.

This eventful mission in Mexico in 1922 coincided with the publication in New York City of Gabriela's first book of poetry, which included the "Sonnets of Death." The appearance of *Desolación* aroused praise and admiration throughout the Spanish-speaking countries and abroad, creating an excitement in the literary world experienced only during the halcyon days of the great Modernists, Rubén Darío, Amado Nervo, and Leopoldo Lugones. In this first book her versification did not differ radically from the metrical structure, rhyme, and stanza forms of these great Spanish American writers. But unlike them, her work did not reflect the influence of the French Parnassians and Symbolists. Her rhythm, music, and imagery were unique; and her own unprecedented diversity of themes appealed to a heterogeneous audience. Even younger poets committed to the new "isms" that proliferated after World War I recognized Gabriela's poetic genius, notwithstanding her loyalty to the forms of a more "conventional" verse.

Desolación included seventy-three poems and a number of poetic writings in prose. The former are grouped under five headings: *Life*, poems on many themes; *School* and *Children*, poems inspired by the teacher's mission and by the child's growing awareness of the world; *Sorrow*, the story of a broken heart; *Nature*, a selective diary of her spiritual widowhood in remote Punta Arenas. The love poems in this first book are "bitter exercises," utterances of complaint, grievances and *venganzas hermosas* ("beautiful vengeances").

Gabriela's second book, *Ternura*, was published in Madrid in 1924, shortly after her residence in Mexico and her first visit to New York. It was a collection of children's poems, including many that had appeared previously in *Desolación*. Over the years, as later editions appeared, she added new material until by 1945 the book included a total of nearly one hundred poems. This collection developed into a genre without precedent in Latin American poetry, and proved Gabriela to be a great innovator in subject, form, and sensibility. This moral and didactic verse with its beauty and occasional humor, exalting children's innocence and their sense of fair play, seemed to inspire the young. Generations of children in the schools of Latin America took it for granted that poetry, however obscure, was fun. Children memorized these verses; grown-ups read them for their own pleasure; composers set them to music for recitation and dance.

After the publication of *Desolación* and *Ternura*, prose works by Gabriela Mistral began to appear with great frequency in the leading newspapers and periodicals of the Americas and Europe, and increasingly she became known for her articles on literature, education, and contemporary events. Her prose, written throughout the second half of her life, is a worthy addition to that heritage of newspaper pieces left by three major Hispanic poets—José Martí, Rubén Darío, and Miguel de Unamuno.

No new collection of poetry appeared until 1938, sixteen years after the publication of her first book, *Desolación*. This new volume, *Tala*, was to reveal a different style, concise and terse, using the colloquial, often archaic speech of the Latin American *pueblo*. The common man was, according to Gabriela, "the best verbal creature made by God." Her rhythm pattern was no longer shaped by the example of the Modernists. Her poetic environment had changed: sackcloth and ashes were nearly absent; hope and a new faith were now evident. To the basic themes of *Desolación* she added recollections of childhood and of her mother's death, hymns to the Andes and the Tropics, and *recados* ("messages") to friends in Chile, Argentina, the Antilles, Mexico, and Spain. The religious crisis of her youth was now replaced by a search for grace. *Tala* was published in Buenos Aires by Sur in April, 1938. Gabriela rushed it to press at a critical moment in the Spanish Civil War as a gift to the Basque children uprooted from their homes. The proceeds of its sale went to children's camps in Catalonia and France.

Some influential Chilean critics who had praised *Desolación* without reserve in the early twenties regretted the absence in *Tala* of certain characteristics of the passionate book of her youth, such as the anguish of love and the obsession with death. Possibly they regretted the fact that Gabriela had ceased to be the last of the romantics, so far as theme was concerned; and in style, she no longer belonged to the Modernists. The younger poets, Pablo Neruda and the disciples of Vincente Huidobro and Pablo de Rokha, who loved and respected *Desolación* as a classic, reacted to *Tala* with great intellectual and emotional excitement. But no one tried to imitate Gabriela's style. Her new metrical simplicity and her idiomatic innovations, inspired by ancient texts and above all by the rural speech of her native valley, made it inimitable.

Lagar, her fourth book, appeared in Chile in 1954, sixteen years after the publication of *Tala* and thirty-two years after *Desolación*. This, her last and possibly greatest book, dealt once again with tragic themes and was filled with deep religious content. It included a group of powerful poems entitled "*Mujeres Locas*" ("Mad Women"), many of which contained elements of autobiography. This book and the earlier *Tala* represent Gabriela's finest work in terms of language, technique, and style, as well as the best expressions of her lifelong quest for religious harmony, brotherhood, spiritual acceptance, and communion with nature and with children.

Introduction by Margaret Bates

When, on November 16, 1945, the newspapers announced the awarding of the Nobel Prize for Literature to a Chilean poet, Gabriela Mistral, the news came as a surprise to many Americans who, though they considered themselves well read, had never heard her name.

The fundamental reason we knew so little of this talented woman who enjoyed a great popularity in the Spanish-speaking world, not only for her words but for her deeds, was because the limited number of her poems translated into English—by heavy hands, for the most part—allowed hardly a glimmer of the real Mistral to shine through. Of course all translation of poetry is difficult, but that of Gabriela particularly so because, like the great Spanish Symbolist poet Antonio Machado, the effect of utter simplicity is backed up by a subtle, complex, hidden machine that extracts from each word, from each sound and accent, its maximum emotional charge. This type of poetry, because of the complexity beneath the surface, is the least translatable.

In the rather garbled newspaper accounts of the award, one important fact was missing: the first edition of Gabriela's first book, *Desolación*, had been published in New York City in 1922 with a dedication by the teachers of Spanish in the United States that expressed the deep admiration and sincere affection which led them to publish her poems. The genesis of this book is explained in its prologue. One evening in February, 1921, Professor Federico de Onís, director of the Spanish Department of Columbia University, read some poems by a Chilean schoolteacher to the assembled teachers and students of Spanish at the Hispanic Institute. Immediately, the rural teacher won the admiration and affection of all those present, for they recognized not only a great literary talent in this new voice of amazing vitality and originality but also a great moral force. Federico de Onís, to whom the book is in great part due, explained the next step: "I had read some of her poems that were reprinted in papers from Spain and I realized, as anyone would realize who read them, that this was a great new poet. They wanted to know where they could get her poems, and all I could give them was a handful of clippings. I told them that if they wanted a volume, enough of them would have to subscribe to copies to pay for the printing. And then I wrote to Gabriela Mistral, who was kind enough to send me what she had."

However, it was not as simple as this statment would lead us to believe. The preface explained the difficulty encountered in securing Gabriela's consent to the collection and publication of her poems. In her "genial modesty" she preferred to leave her work scattered.

The year 1922 was important in the life of Gabriela for another reason. Her trip to Mexico to collaborate with that government's rural education program was the beginning of an international life. While abroad, she often expressed a desire to return to Chile in order to continue her interrupted teaching career and to "raise goats," as she liked to say. But she was never able to resume this work in her native land—work which she began in 1905 when, as Lucila Godoy Alcayaga, at the age of fifteen and without benefit of a teaching certificate, she first became a teacher in an elementary school in La Compañía, a tiny village in the north of Chile near Montegrande, her childhood home.

The rural scenes of that area made a lasting impression on this sensitive child, and all her life she was to carry within her a profound love for these small villages wedged between the immense walls of the Andes, and especially for Montegrande, in the valley of Elqui, where she had her roots. Its rural notes were to sound again and again in her poetry, and the scenes of her childhood were to return to her in remembrances of the subtle aroma of almond trees, her light happy steps as a child, her mother baking bread. Within her she carried the rhythm of the Andean stream that ran through her village—a childhood friend with whom she had long conversations. Natural phenomena in her poems are much more than decorations—they are the protagonists of her dramas. So intimate and familiar was her view of this world that she felt she had created it.

After 1910 Gabriela devoted herself to teaching in secondary schools, having obtained her certificate with the help of a lifelong friend, Pedro Aguirre Cerda, who later became President of Chile. While serving as principal of the *liceo* in Temuco, Gabriela was often visited by a young poet of sixteen, president of the Temuco Literary Club, who was later to become famous as Pablo Neruda. Preceded by her fame as the author of *"Los Sonetos de la Muerte"* ("Sonnets of Death"), Gabriela's arrival caused quite a stir, and she was voted honorary member of Pablo Neruda's literary club. Its members, especially Pablo, were avid readers, and the demands on Gabriela's private library—a very unusual one for a frontier town—were great.

Gabriela had written frequently for her local papers, *La Voz de Elqui* and *El Coquimbo*, when she was teaching in elementary schools near her home town. But her literary fame really dated from 1914 when, as Gabriela Mistral, she was awarded first prize in a national poetry contest in Santiago for the "Sonnets of Death." On December 12, the date of the presentation of the prize, a teacher from the provincial school where Gabriela taught came to express the young poet's regret that she herself could not be present to receive the award. The Chilean poet Victor Domingo Silva read the laureled verses in the absence of the author. Gabriela later confessed that in fact she had been there all the time, watching unnoticed from the balcony, too shy to admit her presence on such an occasion. From that day forward her poems were constantly sought for anthologies and text books.

In spite of her fame as a writer, Gabriela always insisted that she was primarily a teacher. Teaching was her true vocation. Poetry had never been an end in her life. Her poetry was written for the relief of her spirit—to "undo knots." She would agree with her fellow Basque existentialist, Don Miguel de Unamuno, that "the humblest life is worth more than the greatest work of art." Teaching she considered a spiritual maternity. To Gabriela, woman's reason for existence was maternity, material and spiritual. She considered her vocation with the seriousness with which she viewed everything else. In praising the vocation of an eminent Chilean, Carlos Silva Vildósola, she declared that the sacrifice of one's calling is worse than physical suicide. Thomas Hardy knew this well, for in *Jude the Obscure* he considers the sacrifice of vocation a pure tragedy which ends in the victim hanging himself out of desperation. In Gabriela's portrait of "The Rural Teacher," the first virtue she stressed was purity; the teacher must be pure so that she can keep the eyes and the hands of the children of Jesus pure.

When Gabriela left Mexico in 1924 her travels carried her through the United States, France, Spain, Italy, and finally back to Chile where she was named its representative to the Institute of Intellectual Cooperation of the League of Nations in Paris. She taught as a visiting professor for a brief period at Barnard, Mills, Middlebury, Vassar, and the University of Puerto Rico, after which she was named Chilean Consul in Naples, a post she subsequently held in many other parts of the world. It was while serving as Consul of Chile in Petropolis that she was awarded the Nobel Prize. When she heard the news officially, she remarked, "Perhaps it was because I was the candidate of the women and children."

The wide international aspects of Gabriela's life are seen in the cities where the first editions of her books were published— *Desolación*, New York, 1922; *Ternura*, Madrid, 1924; *Tala*, Buenos Aires, 1938; and *Lagar*, Santiago, Chile, 1954. In her preliminary remarks to *Tala* she explained that some circumstance always forced her to publish a book which in her Chilean way she had been putting off until tomorrow. Her first book was published because of the interest of Professor Onís and the teachers of Spanish in the United States. *Tala* was the only material thing the poet had to offer to the Spanish children uprooted and orphaned by the Civil War. She published this book so that the proceeds might go to the homeless Basque children. *Lagar* was published on the occasion of her last visit to Chile, and only because of the strong pressures put upon her by friends there.

Of the four books that Gabriela published in her lifetime, the one that received the most enthusiastic popular acclaim in Latin America was her first book, *Desolación*. Her fellow poets, however, prefer her later books—*Tala* and *Lagar*. In *Desolación*, the torrential emotional life of Gabriela poured forth with all its vehemence. In the very depths of her being she forged her song. It was "a burning dagger thrust into the flesh," an enormous verse with "crests of a fierce ocean." The majesty of its weight wearied her, yet she felt that her tongue was unworthy to sing of its grandeur.

The press felt the fire of this new voice. Manuel de Montoliu wrote from Barcelona: "It seems that Latin America has definitely entered the kingdom of the spirit. The infallible sign of this transcendental fact is the brilliant flash of poetry which shines today across the ocean from the highest peak of the Andes.... Gabriela Mistral is one of those poets with such rich and solid spiritual substance that she does not have time to cultivate form for the sake of form. Her expression is characterized by a volcanic violence and by an enormous synthetic force; her words issue forth candent from an interior forge where they have been hammered into shape in the flames of a mind in perpetual fire. She is one of those poets who has an immense and profound interior world which dictates to her spontaneously the law of exterior beauty; in whom the imagination, the idea, and the physical and spiritual sensibility form one and the same thing with the emotion.... It is understandable how a poet with such gifts must possess an enormous lyric force.... Her lyricism is, in substance, the pure aesthetic emotion of her individual life. Gabriela Mistral is a great lyric poet. She tells us in one of her admirable pieces of prose that 'a song is a wound of love which opened up all things to us.' This definition, one of the most profound that has ever been given of true lyric poetry, contains the essence of the lyricism of our poet."

The distinctive note of *Desolación* is its unique intensity. The muse certainly seems to be the mistral, the fierce, tearing wind of southern France, which like the equally fierce *puelche* of her native Chile, carried everything along with it. The critics who determine value by adherence to rules looked askance at these explosions. But Gabriela, in true Hispanic fashion, turned her back on easy elegance, deliberately eschewed the smooth-flowing, and reveled in the rough-hewn and rugged. A disheveled and burning passion must find its own form. Its muse is not the orderly collected muse of Virgil. Even some of her tender notes are almost ferocious. The dynamic Hispanic genius pays little homage to formal tidiness. The cool-headed poets, content with the resonances of the ivory tower, cannot gain entrance to this hall of the winds, the mistral and the *puelche*, with its primitive earthiness and craggy rural tones. Gabriela's frankness and openness scandalized the routinists.

The vocabulary of Gabriela Mistral is extraordinarily rich and original. Guillermo de Torre, in accordance with the distinction that Leo Spitzer made between the meaning of *habla* ("speech") and *lengua* ("language"), affirmed that it was *habla* and not *lengua* that Gabriela spoke, for speech to her was an individual act of will and intelligence. Marcel Bataillon, author of *Erasme et L'Espagne*, considered Gabriela "one of the greatest Spanish poets of our time," and said that he had found even more reasons to love the Spanish language after reading Gabriela, "whose skill as a poet, a maker of words in the true sense, had once again proved the infinite possibilities of expression Spanish had in the hands of great artists."

Oxford's William J. Entwistle also praised the simplicity and rustic quality of the language of *Tala*. He said that, like Saint Teresa of Avila, Gabriela had created a "rustic revolution" in Spanish by avoiding the bookish speech sanctioned by the Academy. She had the courage to use words that were not in its dictionary. There are other points of similarity in the *habla* of Gabriela and that of Saint Teresa. With the most concrete and homely imagery, both were able to attain great spiritual effects. With their feet planted firmly on the ground, they were able to soar, to create a happy union between the earth and the spirit.

If we interpret *Desolación* as referring to the rent soul of the poet who has lost her lover through suicide, the title would then refer specifically to only one section of the book—"*Dolor*." But the rest of the book contains poems to children, to mothers, poems of a religious nature, and some prose selections. The love Gabriela speaks of in this book is a sober, pure love, serious, bitter, tragic—hence: *Desolación*. In "*Intima*" she tells us that her love is not alone of the body; it is what is in the kiss, yet is not the lips; what breaks the voice, yet is not the breast; it is a wind from God which tears her flesh in passing. It is a "bitter exercise."

Gabriela writes with a dead earnestness and a profound modesty. Hardly ever do we hear a light gay note, a dancing rhythm to balance the gray and black hues of her ardent passion. She differs from other women poets of her time, often painfully self-centered and extremely conscious of their "femininity," in that she seldom mentions herself unless it is to tell us of her plainness. In her poems as in her life she is the arch enemy of *vanitas*.

In the towering strength of her personality she stands high above others. She is profound, for the springs of her inspiration go deep. Her roots are nourished by the first waters of the Hispanic tradition, *el pueblo*, by the Bible, and by the classics of her language. Her *patria* is that great spiritual fatherland which speaks the language of Saint Teresa, Góngora, and Azorín. In this selection of authors, all are included. Azorín, at one extreme, declares that the three essentials the good writer must possess are 1) naturalness, 2) naturalness, 3) naturalness; Góngora, at the other extreme, abandons naturalness for a tortured worked style; Saint Teresa stands for the unique—for Saint Teresa alone.

The scope of Gabriela's interests is immensely broad and profound. With this profundity and breadth there is also elevation, a quality sadly lacking in contemporary poetry. This moral elevation is stressed by practically all the critics. Max Daireaux calls her "a moral influence which works mysteriously on the heart and the mind." Díez Canedo points to Gabriela's "Decalogue of the Artist," where the moral is of more importance than the aesthetic. Pedro Prado says: "You will recognize her for the nobility she awakens." Some have applied to Gabriela her own verses written about Teresa Prats de Sarratea: "when she spoke life became richer, her presence in the world helped to keep it pure."

Don Federico de Onís describes her in this way: "In everything she does she shows a natural superiority and everywhere she leaves a profound impression. She walks with an air of repose, a millenarian serenity; her plaintive, monotonous voice, with its shades of hardness and softness, difficult to imagine, sounds far off; the dolorous contraction of her mouth can turn into a smile of infinite sweetness." Díez Canedo declares that Gabriela "so that she might be more austere in greatness, more refined in sensibility, more religious in emotion, softer in her tenderness, was born a woman." Her physical bearing often belied her inner self. Hernán Díaz Arrieta wondered how such frenzied words could come from such tired lips. Waldo Frank spoke of León Hidalgo's reaction to Gabriela: "He had met Gabriela Mistral, poet of his own Chile: a great dark woman wandering through Europe and always bearing Chile, a mysterious treasure in her fragile hand. He had heard her read her poems in which a fire of her Andes seemed to overwhelm the flowers of the valleys."

It was this quality, together with the happy marriage of the soul and the earth, which gave Gabriela a sense of balance, an aversion to the extremes, which many have pointed out. This steadiness, certainly a rare quality in Hispanic America, can be attributed in part to her Chilean blood with its mixture of Indian and Basque. In speaking of the character of Carlos Silva Vildósola, Gabriela emphasized the importance of the Basque influence in Chilean life: "In the Chilean spirit we see the influence of Basque blood, which has a close approximation to the English character. Up until a few years ago a group of Basque families dominated Chilean life, families which, both in their private and political life, approached more the English type of democracy, slightly grayish in hue, than the spectacular ways of French democracy of '89." She went on to say of this author: "Carlos Silva Vildósola had a marvelous Basque equilibrium which never swayed, a steadiness which resided in the middle of his being and was as stable as the main beam that sustains a house. Once I remarked on this virtue, so uncommon in Hispanic America, and as I write I recall his broad smile as he said, 'Ah, Gabriela, it is the quality least appreciated in our race; the people find it flat and ordinary. In normal times they do not appreciate it, and they only thank one for it when they have been through a storm and need the sensible people, the prudent, to build again the broken body of the shattered state.' It is a sad fact that people consider good sense to be passive. It is active *par excellence*, since it needs to be watched like a burning candle. A little less and it is no longer equanimity—it freezes. Neither frozen nor dull was the equilibrium of this Chilean 'Maestro,' because his whole body hid the hot ashes of a passion so deep that the obtuse could hardly discern it." In this sketch there also lies a self-portrait. But these qualities which Gabriela pointed to in Silva Vildósola she did not recognize in herself. In a poem to a Chilean infant being christened Gabriela, for her, she says she hopes the child will not have her imprudence, that she will not try to thrash the winds or to build beehives for bears.

Along with the Basque influence, that of Arauco is also important in the formation of the austere and virile character of the Chileans. But it is to the Basque influence that Menéndez y Pelayo attributes their artistic limitation: "From its universities came historians, grammarians, economists, and sociologists, rather than poets. The character of the Chilean people, like that of its Basque ancestry is positive, practical, and judicious with little ideality. This artistic limitation is more than compensated by rarer and more useful arts.... But we do not mean *that it will always be so*. God gives birth to the poetic genius all over the world and there is no nation or race which has been disinherited of this divine gift."

It is curious that the country with a weak poetic tradition

gave birth to one of the greatest of Hispanic American poets. It reminds one of Nicaragua and Rubén Darío.

This austere virile attitude, which to Menéndez y Pelayo is characteristic of the Chileans, also shows itself in Gabriela's criticism of the tropical effusiveness which characterizes so much of the literature of the other America. She explained that she chose Ismael Edwards Matte's article about her to serve as the preface for her anthology of selected poems because he had a virtue—rare in a South American author—the English gift of being exact, of not going to extremes of praise or condemnation. When Bolívar overweens in comparing his tribulation to that of the Redeemer, Gabriela had a more fitting comparison: "The glory of Bolívar compared to that of the Redeemer is less than the dirt under my nail."

Although so many speak of Gabriela's passion, not all the poems that poured from the heart of this *"mestiza de vasca"* were cries of anguish. When she asked the sea to bear the wounded body of the voyager smoothly on its waters, she sought serenity and found it. The fire of love and suffering burnt a hole that was black only temporarily; deeper down, there lay the human core untouched, which blossomed forth with a still richer humanity, a soft tenderness and a powerful maternal feeling. This deep maternal affection spiritualized Gabriela's love and penetrated even her view of nature. The tree is the womb, for its branches rock a living being in each light nest.

Her descriptions of nature, very subjective, are always saturated with the dominant mood of the poem. Sometimes her sufferings become more acute because of nature's cold unconcern. At other times she finds in nature a helping hand or a lesson in generosity and understanding. Like Saint Francis, she views nature as the hand of God.

Although at the end of *Desolación* Gabriela apologized for the tragic notes she had uttered, she realized fully the value of suffering, its purifying, cauterizing nature. She asked Christ to make live again the souls of those men which are dead from fear and cold: "Return to them their deep and sensitive soul, give them a house of bitterness, of passion, of lamentation. They will not spit upon you, no, but they are unable to love you. Neither love nor hate moves them. . . . their opaque eyes know not refreshing and cleansing tears. Return to them the fire of their glance!"

Gabriela's creed, as she expressed it in a poem written when she was young, said: "I believe in my own heart." And why? Because it has been created by God who dwells in it, and who will preserve it forever. It thus becomes a symbol of immortality. This theme of Divine Immanence is perhaps the most persistent trait of her religious thought. Throughout her work there is a constant lingering on the thought of death, on immortality, and an acute awareness of the perishableness of the flesh. In her poem *"Viernes Santo"* ("Good Friday"), she writes of the most bitter moment of Christianity—Christ on the Cross. She pleads that no one till the soil or work the plough, for there will be time for work later when hope is returned. "He is still on the wood, a tremendous thirst on His lips; I hate my bread, my happiness; Christ suffers."

The Bible had a profound influence on Gabriela; its strong flavor permeates her poetry. We would expect it to be mentioned first in the list of favorite books of the poet who feels she was born in Israel—the Israel of the Psalms, of the rivers of burning lava that singe her soul, or the gentle Israel hidden in the heart of the Moabitess, Ruth.

But it is Saint Francis who is the source of inspiration for the more tender aspects of her poetry. Her tongue, "parched by the flames of Dante's hell," is refreshed with the dew of the tender meadows of Saint Francis.

In spite of her very active life, solitude—*soledades*—is another dominant note in Gabriela's poetry. She declared that she lived in solitude throughout the world. The mocking heavens are astounded to see a woman so alone. Into this solitude there comes a weariness, a plodding heavy step. The soul refuses to continue pulling the heavy mass of the body along. In *"Nocturno"* ("Nocturn") this terrible weariness comes again and *nails* itself on her eyes. The regular accents on the third, sixth, and ninth syllables lend the poem a fitting monotony of rhythm.

The striking intensity of Gabriela's poetry is attained to a great extent through her constant use of words denoting extreme physical pain—words like scorching, singeing, howling, nailing. Hernán Díaz Arrieta has said that most words sound weak to Gabriela. "She seeks vigor above everything else, and is desperate when she fails to attain it. She twists the language, squeezes it, torments it; she wants to imitate the accent of fire that the Israelites heard and which has remained in the letters of the Old Testament. Nothing matters but that—energy, the maximum of energy. She pulls the chord of the bow until it breaks and the steel arrow takes off with the mad hope of reaching the heart of divinity."

If Gabriela was not a prolific poet, she was a great poet. She was not one to experiment with personae and masks. The same voice speaks throughout her work, whether in the early poems of *Desolación*, the tender, often bitter poems for mothers and children, or the mature poetry of *Tala* and *Lagar*, where her voice is more profound and more sure in recounting experience—its joy, tedium, and tragedy.

This Introduction, originally a talk given by Margaret Bates to Trinity College undergraduates in 1946, has been modified slightly by the editor for this book with the kind permission of Dr. Bates.—D.D.

Translator's Note

If this book helps to bring Gabriela Mistral's poetry to your attention, and if it contributes in any way to your desire to read more of her work, preferably in the original, I shall have accomplished my purpose.

This volume is bilingual because I earnestly hope you will want to read the original Spanish. In his introduction to that remarkable book *The Poem Itself*, Stanley Burnshaw says, "The instant [the reader] departs from the words of the original, he departs from *its* poetry. For the words are the poem. An English translation is always a different thing: it is always an *English* poem." For this reason I urge you to refer back to the original as much as possible, and to read it aloud even if you don't know Spanish. For the poem is also the sound, and that simply cannot be translated.

I have tried for fidelity to the original, above all in tone and content; but I have not bound myself to any precise metrical scheme derived from the Spanish or limited myself by striving for a forced rhyme that cannot be carried over into another language.

In my selection I have endeavored to show many facets of Gabriela's poetry as well as the development of her style and the varied content of her work over the years. I have tried to avoid using poems that have appeared previously in English translation. I would like to have included many more of her works, but space does not permit in one volume.

Texts of the original poems are from *Obras Completas de Gabriela Mistral* (Madrid: Aguilar, 1958), edited by Dr. Margaret

Bates, Professor at the Catholic University of Washington, D.C. I recommend this meticulous work by Dr. Bates to any reader interested in pursuing the original Spanish. It is a definitive edition since Dr. Bates was able to work closely with Gabriela during her last years in my home in Roslyn Harbor, Long Island, and all corrections, deletions, and restorations of verses were made by the poet herself. The volume is complete in the sense that it includes all poems published by Gabriela in book form during her lifetime.

Upon her death Gabriela left a vast amount of unpublished poetry and prose. As heir to these papers, and as executrix for her estate, it has been my responsibility to put them in order, to select, and to publish them. In 1967 I published the first posthumous volume of her poetry, *Poema de Chile* (Santiago: Pomaire), a book of several hundred pages about her native land. A second posthumous book of poems, *Lagar II*, along with several volumes of Gabriela's prose works which I have compiled and edited, will be published soon by Aguilar in Madrid. From *Lagar II* I have translated into English two poems which I include in the pages that follow—"Farewell to a Traveler" (*"Despedida de Viajero"*) and "The Liana" (*"La Liana"*).

Francisco Aguilera, a Chilean, and Dr. Margaret Bates, an American, who contributed the Foreword and Introduction to this volume of selected translations, were personal friends of Gabriela. Both are distinguished for their dedicated work in promoting a better understanding of Hispanic culture—Margaret Bates as a scholar and professor, and Francisco Aguilera for his outstanding and inspired work over the past thirty years in the Hispanic Foundation of the Library of Congress.

As for my own commentaries which precede the four sections, *Desolación*, *Ternura*, *Tala*, and *Lagar*, they are there merely as guideposts. I would like to apply to them what Gabriela said of her own notes for *Tala*. She had written them for the reader, she said, in order "to help him—appearing before him suddenly like an elf, keeping him company on the road for a bit, then disappearing quickly."

I am deeply indebted to the Ford Foundation for its generous assistance in making this book possible; to the Hispanic Foundation of the Library of Congress for its help and support; and above all to its Director, Dr. Howard F. Cline, whose unstinting efforts to bring before the American reader the best of great Latin American culture are well known here and abroad.

I am indebted to the editors of *Atlas Magazine* for permission to include my English translations, "The Liana," "Distribution," "Land of Absence," and "Mourning," and to *Mademoiselle* for permission to reprint "The Disburdened."

I wish to express my deep gratitude to the following persons who have given me so much of their time and help—affording me good counsel, a fine critical eye, and much needed encouragement: Beatriz Engelke, Lila Rosenblum, Phyllis Lintott, and Margit Varga. And here I want to say a special thank you to the memory of Edward T. Dickinson, who in his life was a valued friend of the arts and of Latin America. It was his gentle prodding and kindly encouragement that first got me started on this book.

DORIS DANA

Bridgehampton, Long Island

Desolación DESOLATION 1922

May God forgive me this bitter book, and may those who find life sweet forgive me, too.

Gabriela Mistral wrote these words in 1922 when, under the personal aegis of Professor Federico de Onís of Columbia University, and thanks to the enthusiasm and efforts of the Spanish teachers of the United States, the poetic works of this serious, intense, and dedicated young schoolteacher from Chile appeared for the first time in book form.

Desolación reflects the lonely, majestic landscapes of her native Chile as well as her early years as a rural schoolteacher in the high Andean villages of the valley of Elqui, where she was born, and in the remote desolate towns of Patagonia. This book is passionate, personal, subjective; the pervading tone is tragic. Her voice is sometimes harsh with pain, demanding, austere, as in the many poems of young love and sorrow. At times it is deeply religious—biblical, Hebraic. For children she speaks with a compassionate voice, tender, maternal, often bitter with the awareness of the stark realities of human exploitation and poverty. She includes prose works, too—some are allegorical, lyrical; others, such as "Decalogue of the Artist," are expressions of her beliefs and ideals.

Although many of these works had been written before Gabriela was seventeen, this first volume of poetry placed her among the world's great writers and established her as a voice of profound moral influence. Max Daireaux spoke of this as "not strictly speaking a literary influence: it does not work its effect upon writers but upon men; it is a moral influence which works mysteriously upon the intelligence and the heart and which at first seems inexplicable."

With the publication of *Desolación* in New York City, Gabriela's long relationship with the United States began. She taught in four of our leading colleges and was given honorary degrees by many of our universities including Columbia. Twice she chose the United States as her home, serving as Consul of Chile in California and New York. She was a delegate to the United Nations, served on the Committee for Women's Rights, and played an important part in the founding of UNICEF. At the request of the United Nations in 1946 Gabriela made the first worldwide appeal for funds for the poor children of the world; with this "Appeal for Children" UNICEF came into being. It was in the United States that Gabriela Mistral chose to live the last years of her life, and here she died in 1957, a resident of Roslyn Harbor, Long Island, New York.

D.D.

Palabras Serenas

Ya en la mitad de mis días espigo
esta verdad con frescura de flor:
la vida es oro y dulzura de trigo,
es breve el odio e inmenso el amor.

Mudemos ya por el verso sonriente
aquel listado de sangre con hiel.
Abren violetas divinas, y el viento
desprende al valle un aliento de miel.

Ahora no sólo comprendo al que reza;
ahora comprendo al que rompe a cantar.
La sed es larga, la cuesta es aviesa;
pero en un lirio se enreda el mirar.

Grávidos van nuestros ojos de llanto
y un arroyuelo nos hace sonreír;
por una alondra que erige su canto
nos olvidamos que es duro morir.

No hay nada ya que mis carnes taladre.
Con el amor acabóse el hervir.
Aún me apacienta el mirar de mi madre.
¡Siento que Dios me va haciendo dormir!

Serene Words

Now in the middle of my days I glean
this truth that has a flower's freshness:
life is the gold and sweetness of wheat,
hate is brief and love immense.

Let us exchange for a smiling verse
that verse scored with blood and gall.
Heavenly violets open, and through the valley
the wind blows a honeyed breath.

Now I understand not only the man who prays;
now I understand the man who breaks into song.
Thirst is long-lasting and the hillside twisting;
but a lily can ensnare our gaze.

Our eyes grow heavy with weeping,
yet a brook can make us smile.
A skylark's song bursting heavenward
makes us forget it is hard to die.

There is nothing now that can pierce my flesh.
With love, all turmoil ceased.
The gaze of my mother still brings me peace.
I feel that God is putting me to sleep.

La Espera Inútil

Yo me olvidé que se hizo
ceniza tu pie ligero,
y, como en los buenos tiempos,
salí a encontrarte al sendero.

Pasé valle, llano y río
y el cantar se me hizo triste.
La tarde volcó su vaso
de luz ¡y tú no viniste!

El sol fué desmenuzando
su ardida y muerta amapola;
flecos de niebla temblaron
sobre el campo. ¡Estaba sola!

Al viento otoñal, de un árbol
crujió el blanqueado brazo.
Tuve miedo y te llamé:
"¡Amado, apresura el paso!

"Tengo miedo y tengo amor,
¡amado, el paso apresura!"
Iba espesando la noche
y creciendo mi locura.

Me olvidé de que te hicieron
sordo para mi clamor;
me olvidé de tu silencio
y de tu cárdeno albor;

The Useless Wait

I forgot that your light foot
had turned to ash,
and as in happy times
I set out to meet you on the path.

I crossed valley, plain, and river,
and the singing made me sad.
The evening spilled out its vessel
of light—and you did not come!

The sun crumbled to shreds
like a burnt dead poppy;
flecks of fog trembled
over the fields. I was alone!

From a tree in the autumn wind
came the creaking of a whitened bough.
I was afraid, and I called out to you,
"Beloved, hasten your step!

"I feel fear, and I feel love.
Beloved, hurry to me!"
Night came closing in
and my madness increased.

I forgot they had made you deaf
to my outcry;
I forgot your silence,
your livid pallor.

de tu inerte mano torpe
ya para buscar mi mano;
¡de tus ojos dilatados
del inquirir soberano!

La noche ensanchó su charco
de betún; el agorero
buho con la horrible seda
de su ala rasgó el sendero.

No te volveré a llamar
que ya no haces tu jornada;
mi desnuda planta sigue,
la tuya está sosegada.

Vano es que acuda a la cita
por los caminos desiertos.
¡No ha de cuajar tu fantasma
entre mis brazos abiertos!

I forgot your inert hand,
slow now to seek my hand.
I forgot your eyes staring
wide with the supreme question.

Night spread out its pool
of black pitch; the sorcerer
owl scraped the path with the silken
horror of its wing.

I shall not cry out to you again
since you no longer walk abroad.
My naked foot must travel on,
yours is forever still.

In vain I kept this appointment
on deserted paths.
I cannot bring to life again
your ghost in my open empty arms.

La Espera Inútil

Pasé valle, llano y río
y el cantar se me hizo triste

The Useless Wait

I crossed valley, plain, and river,
and the singing made me sad

Balada

El pasó con otra;
yo le vi pasar.
Siempre dulce el viento
y el camino en paz.
¡Y estos ojos míseros
le vieron pasar!

El va amando a otra
por la tierra en flor.
Ha abierto el espino;
pasa una canción.
¡Y él va amando a otra
por la tierra en flor!

El besó a la otra
a orillas del mar;
resbaló en las olas
la luna de azahar.
¡Y no untó mi sangre
la extensión del mar!

El irá con otra
por la eternidad.
Habrá cielos dulces.
(Dios quiere callar.)
¡Y él irá con otra
por la eternidad!

Ballad

He passed by with another;
I saw him pass by.
The wind ever sweet
and the path full of peace.
And these eyes of mine, wretched,
saw him pass by!

He goes loving another
over the earth in bloom.
The hawthorn is flowering
and a song wafts by.
He goes loving another
over the earth in bloom!

He kissed the other
by the shores of the sea.
The orange-blossom moon
skimmed over the waves.
And my heart's blood did not taint
the expanse of the sea!

He will go with another
through eternity.
Sweet skies will shine.
(God wills to keep silent.)
And he will go with another
through eternity!

Volverlo a Ver

¿Y nunca, nunca más, ni en noches llenas
de temblor de astros, ni en las alboradas
vírgenes, ni en las tardes inmoladas?

¿Al margen de ningún sendero pálido,
que ciñe el campo, al margen de ninguna
fontana trémula, blanca de luna?

¿Bajo las trenzaduras de la selva,
donde llamándolo me ha anochecido,
ni en la gruta que vuelve mi alarido?

¡Oh, no! ¡Volverlo a ver, no importa dónde,
en remansos de cielo o en vórtice hervidor,
bajo unas lunas plácidas o en un cárdeno horror!

¡Y ser con él todas las primaveras
y los inviernos, en un angustiado
nudo, en torno a su cuello ensangrentado!

To See Him Again

And shall it never be again, never? Not on nights filled
with trembling of stars, or by the pure light
of virginal dawns, or on afternoons of immolation?

Never, at the edge of any pale pathway
that borders the field, or beside any
tremulous fountain white under the moon?

Never, beneath the entangled tresses of the forest
where, calling out to him, night descended on me?
Nor in the cavern that returns my echoing outcry?

Oh, no! Just to see him again, no matter where—
in little patches of sky or in the seething vortex,
beneath placid moons or in a livid horror!

And, together with him, to be all springtimes
and all winters, entwined in one anguished knot
around his blood-stained neck!

Dios Lo Quiere

I

La tierra se hace madrastra
si tu alma vende a mi alma.
Llevan un escalofrío
de tribulación las aguas.
El mundo fué más hermoso
desde que me hiciste aliada,
cuando junto de un espino
nos quedamos sin palabras,
¡y el amor como el espino
nos traspasó de fragancia!

Pero te va a brotar víboras
la tierra si vendes mi alma;
baldías del hijo, rompo
mis rodillas desoladas.
Se apaga Cristo en mi pecho
¡y en la puerta de mi casa
quiebra la mano al mendigo
y avienta a la atribulada!

II

Beso que tu boca entregue
a mis oídos alcanza,
porque las grutas profundas
me devuelven tus palabras.
El polvo de los senderos
guarda el olor de tus plantas
y oteándolas como un ciervo,
te sigo por las montañas...

God Wills It

I

The earth will become a hateful stepmother
if your soul should sell my soul.
Waters shudder at the hint
of such suffering.
The world has been more beautiful
since you made me yours,
when beside the thorn tree
we stood wordless,
and love, like a thorn,
pierced us with its fragrance.

But the earth will spew forth serpents
on you if you should sell my soul.
I will shatter the bones of my
desolate knees that rock no child.
The Christ in my heart will die;
at the threshold of my house
He will break the hand of the beggar
and drive away the woman of sorrows.

II

The kiss you give another
will echo in my ears
through deep caverns
that return to me your every word.
Dust of the road
holds the scent of your feet,
and like a deer I shall track you
over the mountains.

A la que tú ames, las nubes
la pintan sobre mi casa.
Ve cual ladrón a besarla
de la tierra en las entrañas;
mas, cuando el rostro le alces,
halles mi cara con lágrimas.

III

Dios no quiere que tú tengas
sol si conmigo no marchas;
Dios no quiere que tú bebas
si yo no tiemblo en tu agua;
no consiente que tú duermas
sino en mi trenza ahuecada.

IV

Si te vas, hasta en los musgos
del camino rompes mi alma;
te muerden la sed y el hambre
en todo monte o llanada
y en cualquier país las tardes
con sangre serán mis llagas.

Y destilo de tu lengua
aunque a otra mujer llamaras,
y me clavo como un dejo
de salmuera en tu garganta;
y odies, o cantes, o ansíes,
¡por mí solamente clamas!

Clouds above my house
will paint the image of the one you love.
Like a thief you will creep
into the deepest corners of the earth to kiss her;
and yet, when you lift up her countenance,
you will find my tear-stained face.

    III

God does not want the sun to shine on you
if you do not walk with me.
God will not let you drink from waters
that do not reflect my face.
God will not let you sleep
except in the hollowed curve of my hair.

    IV

If you leave, you will crush my soul
in the very moss you tread.
Thirst and hunger will gnaw at you
on every mountain and every plain;
and in every land the evening sun
will stain the sky with the blood of my wounds.

My name will burst from your tongue
though you call out to another,
and I will stick like
brine in your throat;
hating or singing or yearning,
it is only for me you will call.

V

Si te vas y mueres lejos,
tendrás la mano ahuecada
diez años bajo la tierra
para recibir mis lágrimas,
sintiendo cómo te tiemblan
las carnes atribuladas,
¡hasta que te espolvoreen
mis huesos sobre la cara!

v

If you leave, and die far from me,
your hand, curved like a cup
beneath the earth, for ten years
will receive my tears.
You will feel the shudder
of my suffering flesh
until my bones crumble
and fall in dust upon your face.

La Oración de la Maestra

¡Señor! Tú que enseñaste, perdona que yo enseñe; que lleve el nombre de maestra, que Tú llevaste por la Tierra.

Dame el amor único de mi escuela; que ni la quemadura de la belleza sea capaz de robarle mi ternura de todos los instantes.

Maestro, hazme perdurable el fervor y pasajero el desencanto. Arranca de mí este impuro deseo de justicia que aún me turba, la mezquina insinuación de protesta que sube de mí cuando me hieren. No me duela la incomprensión ni me entristezca el olvido de las que enseñé.

Dame el ser más madre que las madres, para poder amar y defender como ellas lo que no es carne de mis carnes. Dame que alcance a hacer de una de mis niñas mi verso perfecto y a dejarte en ella clavada mi más penetrante melodía, para cuando mis labios no canten más.

Muéstrame posible tu Evangelio en mi tiempo, para que no renuncie a la batalla de cada día y de cada hora por él.

Pon en mi escuela democrática el resplandor que se cernía sobre tu corro de niños descalzos.

Hazme fuerte, aun en mi desvalimiento de mujer, y de mujer pobre; hazme despreciadora de todo poder que no sea puro, de toda presión que no sea la de tu voluntad ardiente sobre mi vida.

The Teacher's Prayer

Lord, you who taught, forgive me that I teach; forgive me that I bear the name of teacher, the name you bore on earth.

Grant me such devoted love for my school that not even beauty's flame will detract from my faithful tenderness.

Master, make my fervor long-lasting and my disillusion brief. Uproot from me this impure desire for justice that still troubles me, the petty protest that rises up within me when I am hurt. Let not the incomprehension of others trouble me, or the forgetfulness of those I have taught sadden me.

Let me be more maternal than a mother; able to love and defend with all of a mother's fervor the child that is not flesh of my flesh. Grant that I may be successful in molding one of my pupils into a perfect poem, and let me leave within her my deepest-felt melody that she may sing for you when my lips shall sing no more.

Make me strong in my faith that your Gospel is possible in my time, so that I do not renounce the daily battle to make it live.

Let your luminous radiance descend upon my modest school as it did upon the barefoot children who surrounded you.

Make me strong even in my weakness as a woman, and particularly as a poor woman. Make me scorn all power that is not pure, and all duress that is not your flaming will upon my life.

¡Amigo, acompáñame! ¡Sosténme! Muchas veces no tendré sino a Ti a mi lado. Cuando mi doctrina sea más casta y más quemante mi verdad, me quedaré sin los mundanos; pero Tú me oprimirás entonces contra tu corazón, el que supo harto de soledad y desamparo. Yo no buscaré sino en tu mirada la dulzura de las aprobaciones.

Dame sencillez y dame profundidad; líbrame de ser complicada o banal, en mi lección cotidiana.

Dame el levantar los ojos de mi pecho con heridas, al entrar cada mañana a mi escuela. Que no lleve a mi mesa de trabajo mis pequeños afanes materiales, mis mezquinos dolores de cada hora.

Aligérame la mano en el castigo y suavízamela más en la caricia. ¡Reprenda con dolor, para saber que he corregido amando!

Haz que haga de espíritu mi escuela de ladrillos. Le envuelva la llamarada de mi entusiasmo su atrio pobre, su sala desnuda. Mi corazón le sea más columna y mi buena voluntad más oro que las columnas y el oro de las escuelas ricas.

Y, por fin, recuérdame desde la palidez del lienzo de Velázquez, que enseñar y amar intensamente sobre la Tierra es llegar al último día con el lanzazo de Longinos[1] en el costado ardiente de amor.

---

[1] Centurión romano que clavó su lanza en el costado de Cristo agonizante, exclamando despues: "Verdaderamente que este hombre era Hijo de Dios."

Friend, accompany me, sustain me! Many times I will have only you at my side. When my teaching becomes more pure and my truth more burning, the worldly will forsake me; but you will press me to your heart that was so utterly lonely and forsaken. I shall not seek the sweetness of approbation except in your eyes.

Give me simplicity and depth; let me be neither complicated nor commonplace in my everyday teaching.

Each morning when I enter my school, let my vision rise above my own hurt. Let me never carry to my work desk my own small material cares or my personal sorrows.

Let my hand be light in punishment, and my caresses ever more tender. May I reprimand with regret so that I may know I have corrected with love.

Let me make my brick schoolhouse into a spiritual temple. Let the radiance of my enthusiasm envelop the poor courtyard and the bare classroom. Let my heart be a stronger column and my goodwill purer gold than the columns and gold of rich schools.

And, finally, let the pale canvas of Velázquez ever remind me that to teach and to love intensely means to arrive at the last day with the spear of Longinus[1] piercing the heart aflame with love.

[1] The Roman centurion at Calvary who pierced the side of the dying Christ, and who cried out at His death: "Truly, this man was the Son of God."

Piececitos

Piececitos de niño,
azulosos de frío,
¡cómo os ven y no os cubren,
Dios mío!

¡Piececitos heridos
por los guijarros todos,
ultrajados de nieves
y lodos!

El hombre ciego ignora
que por donde pasáis,
una flor de luz viva
dejáis;

que allí donde ponéis
la plantita sangrante,
el nardo nace más
fragante.

Sed, puesto que marcháis
por los caminos rectos,
heroicos como sois
perfectos.

Piececitos de niño,
dos joyitas sufrientes,
¡cómo pasan sin veros
las gentes!

Little Feet

Little feet of children
blue with cold,
how can they see you and not cover you—
dear God!

Little wounded feet
cut by every stone,
hurt by snow
and mire.

Man, blind, does not know
that where you pass,
you leave a flower
of living light.

And where you set
your little bleeding foot,
the spikenard blooms
more fragrant.

Walking straight paths,
be heroic, little feet,
as you are
perfect.

Little feet of children,
two tiny suffering jewels,
how can people pass
and not see you!

El Angel Guardián

Es verdad, no es un cuento;
hay un Angel Guardián
que te toma y te lleva como el viento
y con los niños va por donde van.

Tiene cabellos suaves
que van en la venteada,
ojos dulces y graves
que te sosiegan con una mirada
y matan miedos dando claridad.
(No es un cuento, es verdad.)

El tiene cuerpo, manos y pies de alas
y las seis alas vuelan o resbalan,
las seis te llevan de su aire batido
y lo mismo te llevan de dormido.

Hace más dulce la pulpa madura
que entre tus labios golosos estruja;
rompe a la nuez su taimada envoltura
y es quien te libra de gnomos y brujas.

Es quien te ayuda a que cortes las rosas,
que están sentadas en trampas de espinas,
el que te pasa las aguas mañosas
y el que te sube las cuestas más pinas.

The Guardian Angel

It's true, it isn't a story;
there is a Guardian Angel
who takes you and carries you like the wind
and goes with children wherever children go.

He has soft hair
that blows in the wind.
He has grave sweet eyes
that quiet you with a look
and destroy your fears with their brightness.
(It isn't a story, it's true.)

He has a body, hands and winged feet,
six wings that soar and glide,
six wings that carry you through wing-thrashed air
though you may sleep.

He makes the ripe fruit sweeter
that streams from your honeyed lips;
he cracks the nut from its crafty shell
and sets you free from gnomes and witches.

It is he who helps you cut roses
that sit in a snare of thorns,
and carries you over treacherous waters
and lifts you up the steepest crag.

Y aunque camine contigo apareado,
como la guinda y la guinda bermeja,
cuando su seña te pone el pecado
recoge tu alma y el cuerpo te deja.

Es verdad, no es un cuento:
hay un Angel Guardián
que te toma y te lleva como el viento
y con los niños va por donde van.

Although he goes at your side
like a twin cherry of burnished red,
when sin puts its mark on you,
he abandons your body and gathers up your soul.

It's true, it isn't a story:
there is a Guardian Angel
who takes you and carries you like the wind
and goes with children wherever children go.

A Noel

¡Noel, el de la noche del prodigio,
Noel de barbas caudalosas,
Noel de las sorpresas delicadas
y las pisadas sigilosas!

Esta noche te dejo mi calzado[1]
colgado en los balcones;
antes que hayas pasado por mi casa
no agotes los bolsones.

Noel, Noel, vas a encontrar mojadas
mis medias de rocío,
espiando con ojos picarones
tus barbazas de río...

Sacude el llanto y deja cada una
tiesa, dura y llenita,
con el anillo de la Cenicienta
y el lobo de Caperucita...

Y no olvides a Marta. También deja
su zapatito abierto.
Es mi vecina, y yo la cuido, desde
que su mamita ha muerto.

¡Noel, viejo Noel, de las manazas
rebosadas de dones,
de los ojitos pícaros y azules
y la barba en vellones!...

---

[1] La tradición española es dejar los zapatitos de los niños en la ventana para que los Reyes Magos depositen allí sus regalos.

To Noel

Noel of the marvelous night,
Noel of the tremendous beard,
Noel of delicate surprises
and secret footsteps we cannot hear.

This night I leave you my shoes[1]
set out on the window sill.
Please don't empty your sack
before you pass my house.

Noel, Noel, you will find
my stockings are wet with dew
for my mischievous eyes have been spying
on the river of your beard.

Take away the crying, leave my shoes
firm and hard and full,
stuffed with toys, Cinderella's wedding ring,
Red Riding Hood's wolf.

And there's Martha, don't forget!
She, too, left her empty shoe.
She lives next door, and since her mama died
I look after her.

Old Noel, Noel of big hands
overflowing with gifts,
Noel of twinkling blue eyes
and beard of streaming fleece.

---

[1] The Spanish tradition is that children leave their shoes by the window, and there the Three Kings leave their gifts.

Plegaria por el Nido

Dulce Señor, por un hermano pido
indefenso y hermoso: por el nido!

Florece en su plumilla el trino;
ensaya en su almohadita el vuelo.
¡Y el canto dicen que es divino
y el ala cosa de los cielos!

Dulce tu brisa sea al mecerlo,
mansa tu luna al platearlo,
fuerte tu rama al sostenerlo,
corto el rocío al alcanzarlo.

De su conchita desmañada
tejida con hilacha rubia,
desvía el vidrio de la helada
y las guedejas de la lluvia;

desvía el viento de ala brusca
que lo dispersa a su caricia
y la mirada que lo busca,
toda encendida de codicia...

Tú que me afeas los martirios
dados a tus criaturas finas:
la cabezuela de los lirios
y las pequeñas clavelinas,

guarda su forma con cariño
y caliéntelo tu pasión.
Tirita al viento como un niño
y se parece al corazón.

Prayer for the Nest

Sweet Lord, I pray for my brother,
defenseless and beautiful, I pray for the nest!

Bird songs burst trilling from its feathers;
from its tiny pillow fledglings test their flight.
Song, they say, is a thing of God,
and wings, a thing of heaven.

Let your breeze be soft that rocks it;
gentle your moon that silvers it.
Let your branch that holds it be strong;
brief the morning dew that jewels it.

Ward off the icy frost
and streaming locks of rain
from this helpless shell-like thing
woven from bright ravelings.

Ward off the strong-winged wind
whose caress would shatter it,
and the covetous eye aflame with greed
that seeks it out.

You who scold me for the martyrdom
I gave your most tender creatures—
little heads of marigold
and blossoms of the lily—

Guard its small form with love
and warm it with your passion.
It shivers in the wind like a child,
trembles like a living heart.

Decálogo del Artista

I. Amarás la belleza, que es la sombra de Dios sobre el Universo.

II. No hay arte ateo. Aunque no ames al Creador, lo afirmarás creando a su semejanza.

III. No darás la belleza como cebo para los sentidos, sino como el natural alimento del alma.

IV. No te será pretexto para la lujuria ni para la vanidad, sino ejercicio divino.

V. No la buscarás en las ferias ni llevarás tu obra a ellas, porque la Belleza es virgen, y la que está en las ferias no es Ella.

VI. Subirá de tu corazón a tu canto y te habrá purificado a ti el primero.

VII. Tu belleza se llamará también misericordia, y consolará el corazón de los hombres.

VIII. Darás tu obra como se da un hijo: restando sangre de tu corazón.

IX. No te será la belleza opio adormecedor, sino vino generoso que te encienda para la acción, pues si dejas de ser hombre o mujer, dejarás de ser artista.

X. De toda creación saldrás con vergüenza, porque fué inferior a tu sueño, e inferior a ese sueño maravilloso de Dios, que es la Naturaleza.

Decalogue of the Artist

I.   You shall love beauty, which is the shadow of God over the Universe.

II. There is no godless art. Although you love not the Creator, you shall bear witness to Him creating His likeness.

III. You shall create beauty not to excite the senses but to give sustenance to the soul.

IV. You shall never use beauty as a pretext for luxury and vanity but as a spiritual devotion.

V.   You shall not seek beauty at carnival or fair or offer your work there, for beauty is virginal and is not to be found at carnival or fair.

VI. Beauty shall rise from your heart in song, and you shall be the first to be purified.

VII. The beauty you create shall be known as compassion and shall console the hearts of men.

VIII. You shall bring forth your work as a mother brings forth her child: out of the blood of your heart.

IX. Beauty shall not be an opiate that puts you to sleep but a strong wine that fires you to action, for if you fail to be a true man or a true woman, you will fail to be an artist.

X.   Each act of creation shall leave you humble, for it is never as great as your dream and always inferior to that most marvelous dream of God which is Nature.

Ternura TENDERNESS 1924

Love that stammers, that stutters, is apt to be the love that loves best. That is what my poor love seems like, that I have given to children.

The Cuban writer Jorge Mañach has said that the art of speaking to children is one which only those who have a very deep sense of the spiritual and the concrete can master. Gabriela Mistral, more than any other American poet, with the possible exception of José Martí, mastered that art and brought it to unsurpassed heights of beauty.

Ternura, first published in Madrid, is a collection of Gabriela's poems for mothers and children, many of which had appeared previously in *Desolación*. Her deep sense of the maternal is evident in this book, as is her dedication to a lifelong vocation of teaching. There are beautiful lullabies, which she calls "colloquies the mother holds with her own soul, with her child, and with the Earth Spirit around her, visible by day and audible by night." There are poems that speak to the child's first awareness of the tangible and visible world around him; poems that sing and dazzle the imagination with childhood fantasies; and poems that teach—poems of moralities, sentiments, and attitudes of the heart and spirit that mothers and teachers may pass on to children.

At the time *Ternura* was first published there was no authentic body of children's literature in Latin America. Gabriela tells us that it was still in "swaddling clothes" and that she hoped with this book to encourage its development. She wrote of the great effort that would be required to create such a literature out of folklore—which she called its proper source—an effort especially long and arduous because the "singer of children's songs does not just come into being, but arrives slowly by star routes along which he cannot be hastened."

She created these poems partly to encourage others to write for children, partly to savor again the delights of her own childhood, and partly to serve as a voice for other women. The poet, she tells us, is "an undoer of knots, and love without words is a knot that strangles."

To this day in every classroom throughout Latin America, wherever little children learn to read and write, their voices haltingly pronounce the syllables of these verses. And on every playground from Mexico to Patagonia, Latin American children of all races join hands and form a circle as they dance their *rondas* and sing the lyrics of these poems of *Tenderness*.

D.D.

Meciendo

El mar sus millares de olas
mece, divino.
Oyendo a los mares amantes,
mezo a mi niño.

El viento errabundo en la noche
mece los trigos.
Oyendo a los vientos amantes,
mezo a mi niño.

Dios Padre sus miles de mundos
mece sin ruido.
Sintiendo su mano en la sombra
mezo a mi niño.

Rocking

The sea rocks her thousands of waves.
The sea is divine.
Hearing the loving sea
I rock my son.

The wind wandering by night
rocks the wheat.
Hearing the loving wind
I rock my son.

God, the Father, soundlessly rocks
His thousands of worlds.
Feeling His hand in the shadow
I rock my son.

Meciendo

Oyendo a los mares amantes,
mezo a mi niño

Rocking

Hearing the loving sea
I rock my son

La Madre Triste

Duerme, duerme, dueño mío,
sin zozobra, sin temor,
aunque no se duerma mi alma,
aunque no descanse yo.

Duerme, duerme y en la noche
seas tú menos rumor
que la hoja de la hierba,
que la seda del vellón.

Duerma en ti la carne mía,
mi zozobra, mi temblor.
En ti ciérrense mis ojos:
¡duerma en ti mi corazón!

The Sad Mother

Sleep, sleep, my infant lord,
without fear or trembling at my breast,
though my soul may never slumber,
though my soul may never rest.

Sleep, sleep, and in the night
sleep more silently
than a single blade of grass,
a silken strand of fleece.

In you, my fear, my trembling,
let my body sleep.
Let my eyes close on you,
in you my heart find rest!

Dos Canciones del Zodíaco

I. CANCION DE VIRGO

Un niño tuve al pecho
como una codorniz.
Me adormecí una noche;
no supe más de mí.
Resbaló de mi brazo;
rodó, lo perdí.

Era el niño de Virgo
y del cielo feliz.
Ahora será el hijo
de Luz o Abigail.

Tenía siete cielos;
ahora sólo un país.
Servía al Dios eterno,
ahora a un Kadí.

Sed y hambre no sabía
su boca de jazmín;
ni sabía su muerte.
¡Ahora sí, ahora sí!

Lo busco caminando
del Cenit al Nadir,
y no duermo y me pesa
la noche en que dormí.

Two Songs of the Zodiac

I. SONG OF VIRGO

I had a child at my breast
like a little quail.
One night I fell asleep
and knew nothing more.
He slipped from my arms,
rolled away, and I lost him.

He was the son of Virgo
and of a happy sky.
Now he will be only the son
of a Luz or an Abigail.

Seven heavens were his;
now only one land.
He served Eternal God,
now an earthly judge.

His jasmine mouth
knew neither thirst nor hunger.
He knew nothing of his death.
Now, yes! Now, yes!

I search for him, walking
from zenith to nadir,
and never rest, regretting
that one night I fell asleep.

Me dieron a los Gémines;
yo no los recibí.
Pregunto, y ando, y peno
por ver mi hijo venir.

Ay, vuelva, suba y llegue
derechamente aquí,
o me arrojo del cielo
y lo recobro al fin.

They gave me the Gemini
but I did not accept them.
I ask, I walk, I suffer
to see my son again.

Let him return, let him
climb the skies straight to me,
or let me fling myself from the heavens
to find him at last.

II. CANCION DE TAURUS

El toro carga al niño,
al hombre y la mujer,
y el Toro carga el mundo
con tal que se lo den.

*Búscame por el cielo
y me verás pacer.*

Ahora no soy rojo
como cuando era res.
Subí de un salto al cielo
y aquí me puse a arder.

*A veces soy lechoso,
a veces color miel.*

Arden igual que llamas
mis cuernos y mi piel.
Y arde también mi ruta
hasta el amanecer.

*No duermo ni me apago
para no ser infiel.*

Estuve ya en el Arca,
y en Persia, y en Belén.
Ahora ya no puedo
morir ni envejecer.

II. SONG OF TAURUS

Taurus carries the child,
the man, and the woman.
Taurus carries the world
if they let him.

*Look for me in the heavens
and you will see me grazing.*

Now I am no longer red
as I was when a bull in the field.
In one leap I reached the heavens
and turned to fire.

*Sometimes I'm the color of milk,
sometimes the color of honey.*

My horns and my skin
flame like fire.
The path that I walk
is ablaze until dawn.

*I do not sleep or veil my light
that I may never be faithless.*

I have been in the Ark,
in Persia, and in Bethlehem.
Now I can never die
or grow old again.

Duérmete así lamido
por el Toro de Seth.

Dormido irás creciendo;
creciendo harás la Ley
y escogerás ser Cristo
o escogerás ser Rey.

Hijito de Dios Padre
en brazos de mujer.

Sleep, little one, licked
by the bull of Seth.

Sleeping, you will grow;
growing, you will write the Law.
And you will choose to be King
or you will choose Christ, the Lord.

Little son of God the Father,
asleep in the arms of woman.

Apegado a Mí

Velloncito de mi carne,
que en mi entraña yo tejí,
velloncito friolento,
¡duérmete apegado a mí!

La perdiz duerme en el trébol
escuchándole latir:
no te turben mis alientos,
¡duérmete apegado a mí!

Hierbecita temblorosa
asombrada de vivir,
no te sueltes de mi pecho:
¡duérmete apegado a mí!

Yo que todo lo he perdido
ahora tiemblo de dormir.
No resbales de mi brazo:
¡duérmete apegado a mí!

Close to Me

Little fleece of my flesh
that I wove in my womb,
little shivering fleece,
sleep close to me!

The partridge sleeps in the clover
hearing its heart beat.
My breathing will not wake you.
Sleep close to me!

Little trembling blade of grass
astonished to be alive,
don't leave my breast.
Sleep close to me!

I who have lost everything
am now afraid to sleep.
Don't slip away from my arms.
Sleep close to me!

Canción Amarga

¡Ay! ¡Juguemos, hijo mío,
a la reina con el rey!

Este verde campo es tuyo.
¿De quién más podría ser?
Las alfalfas temblorosas
para tí se han de mecer.

Este valle es todo tuyo.
¿De quién más podría ser?
Para que los disfrutemos
los pomares se hacen miel.

(¡Ay! ¡No es cierto que tiritas
como el Niño de Belén
y que el seno de tu madre
se secó de padecer!)

El cordero está espesando
el vellón que he de tejer.
Y son tuyas las majadas.
¿De quién más podrían ser?

Y la leche del establo
que en la ubre ha de correr,
y el manojo de las mieses,
¿de quién más podrían ser?

Bitter Song

Let us play, my son,
at being king and queen.

This green field is yours,
whose else could it be?
Waving fields of alfalfa
are cradle-rocked for you.

This whole valley is yours.
Whose else could it be?
For your joy and mine
orchards give apple-honey.

(No! It is not true that you shiver
like the Child of Bethlehem,
and that the breasts of your mother
are dry with suffering.)

The sheep is growing thick fleece
for wool that I must weave.
Sheep and pasture are yours.
Whose else could they be?

Sweet milk in the stables
flowing from udders,
and the gleanings of harvest,
whose else could they be?

(¡Ay! ¡No es cierto que tiritas
como el Niño de Belén
y que el seno de tu madre
se secó de padecer!)

¡Sí! ¡Juguemos, hijo mío,
a la reina con el rey!

(No! It is not true that you shiver
like the Child of Bethlehem,
and that the breasts of your mother
are dry with suffering.)

Yes! Let us play, my son,
at being king and queen!

Con Tal Que Duermas

La rosa colorada
cogida ayer;
el fuego y la canela
que llaman clavel;

el pan horneado
de anís con miel,
y el pez de la redoma
que la hace arder:

todito tuyo
hijito de mujer,
con tal que quieras
dormirte de una vez.

La rosa, digo:
digo el clavel.
La fruta, digo,
y digo que la miel;

y el pez de luces
y más y más también,
¡con tal que duermas
hasta el amanecer!

If You'll Only Go To Sleep

The crimson rose
plucked yesterday,
the fire and cinnamon
of the carnation,

the bread I baked
with anise seed and honey,
and the goldfish
flaming in its bowl.

All these are yours,
baby born of woman,
if you'll only
go to sleep.

A rose, I say!
And a carnation!
Fruit, I say!
And honey!

And a sequined goldfish,
and still more I'll give you
if you'll only sleep
till morning.

Niño Mexicano

Estoy en donde no estoy,
en el Anáhuac plateado,
y en su luz como no hay otra
peino un niño de mis manos.

En mis rodillas parece
flecha caída del arco,
y como flecha lo afilo
meciéndolo y canturreando.

En luz tan vieja y tan niña
siempre me parece hallazgo,
y lo mudo y lo volteo
con el refrán que le canto.

Me miran con vida eterna
sus ojos negri-azulados,
y como en costumbre eterna,
yo lo peino de mis manos.

Resinas de pino-ocote
van de su nuca a sus brazos,
y es pesado y es ligero
de ser la flecha sin arco...

Lo alimento con un ritmo,
y él me nutre de algún bálsamo
que es el bálsamo del maya
del que a mí me despojaron.

Mexican Child

I am where I am not,
on the silvery Anáhuac,
and by its light, since there is no other,
I comb a little boy's hair with my hands.

On my knees he is like
an arrow fallen from a bow,
and I sharpen him like an arrow,
rocking him to and fro.

In a light so old and so young,
he seems always newly found,
and I change him and turn him
with the refrain that I sing.

His black-blue eyes gaze at me
with eternal life,
and, in the eternal custom,
I comb him with my hands.

Resin of pitch-pine trickles
from his neck to his arms,
and he is both heavy and light,
being an arrow without a bow . . .

I feed him with rhythm
and he nourishes me with balm,
balsam of the Mayas
from whom I was exiled.

Yo juego con sus cabellos
y los abro y los repaso,
y en sus cabellos recobro
a los mayas dispersados.

Hace dos años dejé
a mi niño mexicano;
pero despierta o dormida
yo lo peino de mis manos ...

¡Es una maternidad
que no me cansa el regazo,
y es un éxtasis que tengo
de la gran muerte librado!

And I play with his hair,
part it, caress it,
and in his hair I find again
my lost dispersed Mayas.

Two years ago I left
my little Mexican boy,
but awake or asleep
I comb him with my hands.

It is a maternity
that never tires my lap.
It is an ecstasy I live
freed from great death!

Miedo

Yo no quiero que a mi niña
golondrina me la vuelvan.
Se hunde volando en el cielo
y no baja hasta mi estera;
en el alero hace nido
y mis manos no la peinan.
Yo no quiero que a mi niña
golondrina me la vuelvan.

Yo no quiero que a mi niña
la vayan a hacer princesa.
Con zapatitos de oro
¿cómo juega en las praderas?
Y cuando llegue la noche
a mi lado no se acuesta . . .
Yo no quiero que a mi niña
la vayan a hacer princesa.

Y menos quiero que un día
me la vayan a hacer reina.
La pondrían en un trono
a donde mis pies no llegan.
Cuando viniese la noche
yo no podría mecerla . . .
¡Yo no quiero que a mi niña
me la vayan a hacer reina!

Fear

I don't want them to turn
my little girl into a swallow.
She would fly far away into the sky
and never fly again to my straw bed,
or she would nest in the eaves
where I could not comb her hair.
I don't want them to turn
my little girl into a swallow.

I don't want them to make
my little girl a princess.
In tiny golden slippers
how could she play on the meadow?
And when night came, no longer
would she sleep at my side.
I don't want them to make
my little girl a princess.

And even less do I want them
one day to make her queen.
They would put her on a throne
where I could not go to see her.
And when nighttime came
I could never rock her . . .
I don't want them to make
my little girl a queen!

Suavidades

Cuando yo te estoy cantando,
en la Tierra acaba el mal:
todo es dulce por tus sienes:
la barranca, el espinar.

Cuando yo te estoy cantando,
se me acaba la crueldad:
suaves son, como tus párpados,
¡la leona y el chacal!

Serenity

When I am singing to you,
on earth all evil ends:
as smooth as your forehead
are the gulch and the bramble.

When I am singing to you,
for me all cruel things end:
as gentle as your eyelids,
the lion with the jackal.

La Casa

La mesa, hijo, está tendida,
en blancura quieta de nata,
y en cuatro muros azulea,
dando relumbres, la cerámica.
Esta es la sal, éste el aceite
y al centro el Pan que casi habla.
Oro más lindo que oro del Pan
no está ni en fruta ni en retama,
y da su olor de espiga y horno
una dicha que nunca sacia.
Lo partimos, hijito, juntos,
con dedos duros y palma blanda,
y tú lo miras asombrado
de tierra negra que da flor blanca.

Baja la mano de comer,
que tu madre también la baja.
Los trigos, hijo, son del aire,
y son del sol y de la azada;
pero este Pan "cara de Dios"*
no llega a mesas de las casas;
y si otros niños no lo tienen,
mejor, mi hijo, no lo tocaras,
y no tomarlo mejor sería
con mano y mano avergonzadas.

* En Chile, el pueblo llama al pan "cara de Dios." (G.M.)

The House

The table, son, is laid
with the quiet whiteness of cream,
and on four walls ceramics
gleam blue, glint light.
Here is the salt, here the oil,
in the center, bread that almost speaks.
Gold more lovely than gold of bread
is not in broom plant or fruit,
and its scent of wheat and oven
gives unfailing joy.
We break bread, little son, together
with our hard fingers, our soft palms,
while you stare in astonishment
that black earth brings forth a white flower.

Lower your hand that reaches for food
as your mother also lowers hers.
Wheat, my son, is of air,
of sunlight and hoe;
but this bread, called "the face of God,"*
is not set on every table.
And if other children do not have it,
better, my son, that you not touch it,
better that you do not take it
with ashamed hands.

     *In Chile, the people call bread "the face of God." (G.M.)

Hijo, el Hambre, cara de mueca,
en remolino gira las parvas,
y se buscan y no se encuentran
el Pan y el Hambre corcovada.
Para que lo halle, si ahora entra,
el Pan dejemos hasta mañana;
el fuego ardiendo marque la puerta,
que el indio quechua nunca cerraba,
¡y miremos comer al Hambre,
para dormir con cuerpo y alma!

My son, Hunger with his grimaced face
in eddies circles the unthrashed wheat.
They search and never find each other,
Bread and hunchbacked Hunger.
So that he find it if he should enter now,
we'll leave the bread until tomorrow.
Let the blazing fire mark the door
that the Quechuan Indian never closed,
and we will watch Hunger eat
to sleep with body and soul.

La Casa

La mesa, hijo, está tendida,
en blancura quieta da nata

The House

The table, son, is laid
with the quiet whiteness of cream

Tala FELLING 1938

I will leave behind me the dark ravine, and climb up gentler slopes toward that spiritual mesa where at last a wide light will fall upon my days. From there I will sing words of hope, without looking into my heart. As one who was full of compassion wished: I will sing to console men.

This was the promise Gabriela made in her epilogue to *Desolación*. Sixteen years later the publication of *Tala*, a work still richer and more varied, in part fulfilled that promise.

It has been said that going from *Desolación* to *Tala* is like moving from the Old Testament to the Gospels. Professor Margot Arce de Vázquez in her book *Gabriela Mistral: The Poet and Her Work* (New York: New York University Press, 1964) says that it may be "likened to entering the illuminating state of mysticism after leaving behind the asperities of asceticism." The word *tala* itself means the felling of trees, the chopping down of trees at their roots to make the ground smooth, to clear the dense forest. And certainly we find here a gentler voice, filled with new hope, with an intense searching after grace, at times ecstatic.

This book was written over the long span of years between 1922 and 1938, during which time Gabriela lived for the most part in Europe—in Paris where she worked with Madame Curie and Henri Bergson in the League of Nations; in Madrid, Lisbon, and Marseilles, where she served as honorary Consul of Chile and earned her living writing articles for many newspapers of the world; and in the small towns of the Ligurian coast, where the beauty of Italy and the warmth of the Italian people helped to bring her a new kind of peace and a spiritual joy that radiates from the happier poems in this book.

In *Tala* there is a continuity of the old themes found in *Desolación*—death, grief, children, religious faith, nature, the ecstatic encounter with familiar everyday things, the mystery of the imponderable world of the spirit. Among new themes introduced are the solitude and loneliness of the wanderer, as expressed in "The Foreigner" ("*La Extranjera*"), written in Provence, and in that haunting poem full of lyricism and the ineffable, "Land of Absence" ("*País de la Ausencia*"). At the same time there is a rising eulogy for the Americas, for their noble mountains, their austere regions of ice and desert, their coasts and oceans and sunny islands. Germán Arciniegas says of Gabriela in *Latin America: A Cultural History* (New York: Knopf, 1966), "she carried the human substance of America, at once magical and biblical, in her spirit and her very bones. She moved through Europe like a somnambulist, possessed by the spirit of her native land."

If there is a new tone, a new accent in *Tala*, it must also be said that the voice—vigorous, delicate, original—is essentially the same. And despite the new note of hope, when pain and grief strike her, as upon the death of her mother, her voice recovers its old anguish. Gabriela herself says in her notes at the end of the volume: "This book carries within it a small residue of *Desolación*. And the book that will follow—if one follows—will also carry a residue of *Tala*. So it happens in my valley of Elqui with the pressing of grapes. Fruits remain in the crevices of the baskets and are found later by the vintagers. But the wine has already been made so they leave this residue for the next round of baskets...."

D.D.

País de la Ausencia

País de la ausencia,
extraño país,
más ligero que ángel
y seña sutil,
color de alga muerta,
color de neblí,
con edad de siempre,
sin edad feliz.

No echa granada,
no cría jazmín,
y no tiene cielos
ni mares de añil.
Nombre suyo, nombre,
nunca se lo oí,
y en país sin nombre
me voy a morir.

Ni puente ni barca
me trajo hasta aquí,
no me lo contaron
por isla o país.
Yo no lo buscaba
ni lo descubrí.

Parece una fábula
que yo me aprendí,
sueño de tomar
y de desasir.
Y es mi patria donde
vivir y morir.

Land of Absence

Land of absence,
strange land,
lighter than angel
or subtle sign,
color of dead algae,
color of falcon,
with the age of all time,
with no age content.

It bears no pomegranate
nor grows jasmin,
and has no skies
nor indigo seas.
Its name, a name
that has never been heard,
and in a land without name
I shall die.

Neither bridge nor boat
brought me here.
No one told me
it was island or shore.
A land I did not search for
and did not discover.

Like a fable
that I learned,
a dream of taking
and letting go,
and it is my land
where I live and I die.

Me nació de cosas
que no son país;
de patrias y patrias
que tuve y perdí;
de las criaturas
que yo vi morir;
de lo que era mío
y se fué de mí.

Perdí cordilleras
en donde dormí;
perdí huertos de oro
dulces de vivir;
perdí yo las islas
de caña y añil,
y las sombras de ellos
me las vi ceñir
y juntas y amantes
hacerse país.

Guedejas de nieblas
sin dorso y cerviz,
alientos dormidos
me los vi seguir,
y en años errantes
volverse país,
y en país sin nombre
me voy a morir.

It was born to me of things
that are not of land,
of kingdoms and kingdoms
that I had and I lost,
of all things living
that I have seen die,
of all that was mine
and went from me.

I lost ranges of mountains
wherein I could sleep.
I lost orchards of gold
that were sweet to live.
I lost islands of indigo
and sugar cane,
and the shadows of these
I saw circling me,
and together and loving
become a land.

I saw manes of fog
without back or nape,
saw sleeping breaths
pursue me,
and in years of wandering
become a land,
and in a land without name
I shall die.

La Medianoche

Fina, la medianoche.
Oigo los nudos del rosal:
la savia empuja subiendo a la rosa.

Oigo
las rayas quemadas del tigre
real: no le dejan dormir.

Oigo
la estrofa de uno,
y le crece en la noche
como la duna.

Oigo
a mi madre dormida
con dos alientos.
(Duermo yo en ella,
de cinco años.)

Oigo el Ródano
que baja y que me lleva como un padre
ciego de espuma ciega.

Y después nada oigo
sino que voy cayendo
en los muros de Arlés
llenos de sol . . .

Midnight

Delicate, the midnight.
I hear the nodes of the rosebush:
upthrust of sap ascending to the rose.

I hear
the scorched stripes of the royal tiger:
they do not let him sleep.

I hear
the verse of someone.
It swells in the night
like a dune.

I hear
my mother sleeping,
breathing two breaths.
(In her I sleep,
a child of five.)

I hear the Rhone's rush
that falls and carries me like a father
blind with blind foam.

And then I hear nothing,
but am falling, falling
among the walls of Arles
resplendent with sun ...

Todas Ibamos a Ser Reinas

Todas íbamos a ser reinas,
de cuatro reinos sobre el mar:
Rosalía con Efigenia
y Lucila[1] con Soledad.

En el valle de Elqui, ceñido
de cien montañas o de más,
que como ofrendas o tributos
arden en rojo y azafrán.

Lo decíamos embriagadas,
y lo tuvimos por verdad,
que seríamos todas reinas
y llegaríamos al mar.

Con las trenzas de los siete años,
y batas claras de percal,
persiguiendo tordos huidos
en la sombre del higueral.

De los cuatro reinos, decíamos,
indudables como el Korán,
que por grandes y por cabales
alcanzarían hasta el mar.

Cuatro esposos desposarían,
por el tiempo de desposar,
y eran reyes y cantadores
como David, rey de Judá.

---

[1] En estos versos *Lucila* es Gabriela misma. Las otras tres niñas son sus compañeras en la pequeña escuela de Montegrande.

We Were All To Be Queens

We were all to be queens
of four kingdoms on the sea:
Efigenia with Soledad,
and Lucila[1] with Rosalie.

In the Valley of Elqui, encircled
by a hundred mountains or more
that blaze red like burnished offerings
or tributes of saffron ore,

We said it, enraptured,
and believed it perfectly,
that we would all be queens
and would one day reach the sea.

With our braids of seven-year-olds
and bright aprons of percale,
chasing flights of thrushes
among the shadows of vine and grape.

And our four kingdoms, we said,
so vast and great would be,
that as certain as the Koran
they would all reach the sea.

We would wed four husbands
at the time when we should wed,
and they would all be kings and poets
like King David of Judea.

---

[1] In this poem *Lucila* is Gabriela herself. The other three little girls are her childhood companions in the one-room schoolhouse in Montegrande.

Y de ser grandes nuestros reinos,
ellos tendrían, sin faltar,
mares verdes, mares de algas,
y el ave loca del faisán.

Y de tener todos los frutos,
árbol de leche, árbol del pan,
el guayacán no cortaríamos
ni morderíamos metal.

Todas íbamos a ser reinas,
y de verídico reinar;
pero ninguna ha sido reina
ni en Arauco ni en Copán . . .

Rosalía besó marino
ya desposado con el mar,
y al besador, en las Guaitecas,
se lo comió la tempestad.

Soledad crió siete hermanos
y su sangre dejó en su pan,
y sus ojos quedaron negros
de no haber visto nunca el mar.

En las viñas de Montegrande,
con su puro seno candeal,
mece los hijos de otras reinas
y los suyos nunca-jamás.

Our kingdoms would be so vast
they would have, without a doubt,
green seas, and seas of algae
and wild pheasant.

Our lands would be so fruitful,
trees of milk, trees of bread,
that we would never cut the guaiacum
or eat the earth's metal.

We were all to be queens
and we would truly reign,
but not one of us has been a queen
even in Arauco or Copan.

Rosalie kissed a sailor
already wedded to the sea,
and in Guaitecas the one who kissed her
was devoured by the storm.

Soledad reared seven brothers
and left her life-blood in the bread,
and her eyes have remained forever black
for never having looked on the sea.

In the vineyards of Montegrande,
on her pure and faithful breast
she rocks the sons of other queens,
and never her own—never.

Efigenia cruzó extranjero
en las rutas, y sin hablar,
le siguió, sin saberle nombre,
porque el hombre parece el mar.

Y Lucila, que hablaba a río,
a montaña y cañaveral,
en las lunas de la locura
recibió reino de verdad.

En las nubes contó diez hijos
y en los salares su reinar,
en los ríos ha visto esposos
y su manto en la tempestad.

Pero en el valle de Elqui, donde
son cien montañas o son más,
cantan las otras que vinieron
y las que vienen cantarán:

"En la tierra seremos reinas,
y de verídico reinar,
y siendo grandes nuestros reinos,
llegaremos todas al mar."

Efigenia met a stranger
on the road, and wordlessly
she followed him, nor knew his name,
for a man is like the sea.

And Lucila who talked with the river
and the mountain and fields of cane,
under moons of madness
received a kingdom of her own.

In the clouds she counted ten sons,
and over the salt marsh she reigned,
in the rivers she saw her husbands
and in the tempest, her royal train.

But in the valley of Elqui,
among a hundred mountains or more,
others have come and are singing
and there will sing many more:

"On the earth we will be queens
and we shall truly reign,
and our kingdoms will be so vast
we will all reach the sea."

Riqueza

Tengo la dicha fiel
y la dicha perdida:
la una como rosa,
la otra como espina.
De lo que me robaron
no fuí desposeída:
tengo la dicha fiel
y la dicha perdida,
y estoy rica de púrpura
y de melancolía.
¡Ay, qué amada es la rosa
y qué amante la espina!
Como el doble contorno
de las frutas mellizas,
tengo la dicha fiel
y la dicha perdida...

Richness

I have a faithful joy
and a joy that is lost.
One is like a rose,
the other, a thorn.
The one that was stolen
I have not lost.
I have a faithful joy
and a joy that is lost.
I am as rich with purple
as with sorrow.

Ay! How loved is the rose,
how loving the thorn!
Paired as twin fruit,
I have a faithful joy
and a joy that is lost.

Jugadores

Jugamos nuestra vida
y bien se nos perdió.
Era robusta y ancha
como montaña al sol.

Y se parece al bosque
raído, y al dragón
cortado, y al mar seco,
y a ruta sin veedor.

La jugamos por nuestra,
como sangre y sudor,
y era para la dicha
y la Resurrección.

Otros jugaban dados,
otros colmado arcón;
nosotros los frenéticos,
jugamos lo mejor.

Fué más fuerte que vino
y que agua de turbión
ser en la mesa el dado
y ser el jugador.

Creímos en azares,
en el *sí* y en el *no*.
Jugábamos, jugando,
infierno y salvación.

Gamblers

We gambled our life
and then lost it.
It was robust and wide
as a mountain in the sun.

Now it is razed woods,
slashed dragon,
dry sea, a path
that no one beholds.

We gambled our life as if
it were ours, like blood and sweat.
It was intended
for joy and Resurrection.

Some played at dice,
others at treasure chest.
We, the frenetic,
played the game that was best.

More potent than wine,
stronger than cloudburst,
to be at the table
both the stakes and the gambler.

We believed in chance,
believed in *yes* and *no*.
Gambling, we gambled
hell and salvation.

No nos guarden la cara,
la marcha ni la voz;
ni nos hagan fantasma
ni nos vuelvan canción.

Ni nombre ni semblante
guarden del jugador.
¡Volveremos tan nuevos
como ciervo y alción!

Si otra vez asomamos,
si hay segunda ración,
traer, no traeremos
cuerpo de jugador.

Do not remember our face,
our walk or our voice.
Do not turn us into ghosts
or sing of us in song.

Do not keep the name
or the face of the gambler.
We shall return totally new
as a deer or halcyon.

If we should come here again,
if there should be a second chance,
we won't bring again
the body of a gambler.

La Extranjera

Habla con dejo de sus mares bárbaros,
con no sé qué algas y no sé qué arenas;
reza oración a dios sin bulto y peso,
envejecida como si muriera.
En huerto nuestro que nos hizo extraño,
ha puesto cactus y zarpadas hierbas.
Alienta del resuello del desierto
y ha amado con pasión de que blanquea,
que nunca cuenta y que si nos contase
sería como el mapa de otra estrella.
Vivirá entre nosotros ochenta años,
pero siempre será como si llega,
hablando lengua que jadea y gime
y que le entienden sólo bestezuelas.
Y va a morirse en medio de nosotros,
en una noche en la que más padezca,
con sólo su destino por almohada,
de una muerte callada y *extranjera*.

The Foreigner

She speaks with the moisture of her barbarous seas
still on her tongue, with the taste
of sands and algae unknown to me.
She prays to a god without form or weight,
and is so old she is ready to die.
In our garden which has become strange to us
she grows cactus and clawing grass.
She was nourished by breath of the desert
and loved with a scorching passion
she never tells. If she told us,
it would be like the map of another star.
She will live with us eighty years,
always as if just arriving,
speaking a language that pants and moans
and that only little beasts understand.
And she will die among us
on a night when she suffers most,
only her fate for a pillow,
a death silent and *foreign*.

Canción de las Muchachas Muertas[1]

¿Y las pobres muchachas muertas,
escamoteadas en abril,
las que asomáronse y hundiéronse
como en las olas el delfín?

¿Adónde fueron y se hallan,
encuclilladas por reír
o agazapadas esperando
voz de un amante que seguir?

¿Borrándose como dibujos
que Dios no quiso reteñir
o anegadas poquito a poco
como en sus fuentes un jardín?

A veces quieren en las aguas
ir componiendo su perfil,
y en las carnudas rosas-rosas
casi consiguen sonreír.

En los pastales acomodan
su talle y bulto de ceñir
y casi logran que una nube
les preste cuerpo por ardid;

casi se juntan las deshechas;
casi llegan al sol feliz;
casi reniegan su camino
recordando que eran de aquí;

[1] Gabriela dedicó esta poema a su sobrina Graciela quien murió muy joven.

Song of the Dead Maidens[1]

And the poor dead girls who in April
vanished at the trick of a hand,
those who peeked out and submerged again
like dolphins among the waves?

Where did they go? Where can we find them
crouched on their heels, rocking with laughter,
or hiding, waiting the voice
of a lover they long to follow?

Were they erased like pictures
that God would not color again?
Or immersed, little by little,
like a garden by brooks and rain?

At times they yearn to reshape
their fleeting profiles in water,
and in profusion and flesh of roses
almost break into smile.

They alter their tremulous forms
to the girth of plant and sapling,
and almost beguile a cloud
into lending them shape and body.

They almost mend their shattered selves,
almost burst out to a joyous sun,
they almost renounce their journey
remembering where they were from.

[1] Dedicated by Gabriela to her niece Graciela who died very young.

casi deshacen su traición
y van llegando a su redil.
¡Y casi vemos en la tarde
el divino millón venir!

They almost undo their betrayal
and almost regain the fold.
In the afternoon skies we can almost see
millions of maidens approach.

La Flor del Aire*

Yo la encontré por mi destino,
de pie a mitad de la pradera,
gobernadora del que pase,
del que le hable y que la vea.

Y ella me dijo: "Sube al monte.
Yo nunca dejo la pradera,
y me cortas las flores blancas
como nieves, duras y tiernas."

Me subí a la ácida montaña,
busqué las flores donde albean,
entre las rocas existiendo
medio dormidas y despiertas.

Cuando bajé, con carga mía,
la hallé a mitad de la pradera,
y fuí cubriéndola frenética,
con un torrente de azucenas.

Y sin mirarse la blancura,
ella me dijo: "Tú acarrea
ahora sólo flores rojas.
Yo no puedo pasar la pradera."

Trepé las peñas con el venado,
y busqué flores de demencia,
las que rojean y parecen
que de rojez vivan y mueran.

* "La Aventura" quise llamarla; mi aventura con la Poesía. (G.M.)

The Flower of Air*

I met her, not by chance,
standing in the middle of the meadow,
governing all who passed,
all who addressed her.

She said to me: "Climb the mountain—
I never leave the meadow.
Cut me flowers white
as snows, crisp and tender."

I climbed the mountain
and searched where flowers whiten
among the rocks,
half sleeping, half waking.

When I came down with my burden
I found her in the middle of the meadow.
Like a crazy one, I covered her
with a deluge of lilies.

She never glanced at their whiteness.
She said to me: "Now bring me
red flowers, only the red.
I cannot leave the meadow."

I clambered up crags with deer
and searched for flowers of madness,
those that grow red and appear
to live and die of redness.

    * I wanted to call this "The Adventure," my adventure with Poetry. (G.M.)

Cuando bajé se las fuí dando
con un temblor feliz de ofrenda,
y ella se puso como el agua
que en ciervo herido se ensangrienta.

Pero mirándome, sonámbula,
me dijo: "Sube y acarrea
las amarillas, las amarillas.
Yo nunca dejo la pradera."

Subí derecho a la montaña
y me busqué las flores densas,
color de sol y de azafranes,
recién nacidas y ya eternas.

Al encontrarla, como siempre,
a la mitad de la pradera,
segunda vez yo fuí cubriéndola,
y la dejé como las eras.

Y todavía, loca de oro,
me dijo: "Súbete, mi sierva,
y cortarás las sin color,
ni azafranadas ni bermejas.

"Las que yo amo por recuerdo
de la Leonora y la Ligeia,[1]
color del Sueño y de los sueños.
Yo soy Mujer de la pradera."

[1] Personajes en la obra de Edgar Allan Poe.

When I came down, I offered them
in trembling tribute;
she became red as water bloodied
by the wounded deer.

She gazed at me, half dreaming,
and said: "Go climb again and bring me
the yellow, only the yellow.
I never leave the meadow."

I went straightway to the mountain
and searched for clustered flowers,
color of sun, color of saffron,
newly born, already eternal.

When I returned, I found her still standing
in the middle of the meadow.
I showered her with sun-burst blossoms
till she was golden as the threshing floor.

And once again, crazy with gold,
she said: "Go up, my servant,
and cut flowers that have no color,
not saffron, not burnished red.

"Bring me flowers that I love,
remembering Eleonora and Ligeia,[1]
flowers color of dream, color of dreaming.
I am the woman of the meadow."

[1] Characters in the works of Edgar Allan Poe.

Me fuí ganando la montaña,
ahora negra como Medea,
sin tajada de resplandores,
como una gruta vaga y cierta.

Ellas no estaban en las ramas,
ellas no abrían en las piedras
y las corté del aire dulce,
tijereteándolo ligera.

Me las corté como si fuese
la cortadora que está ciega.
Corté de un aire y de otro aire,
tomando el aire por mi selva...

Cuando bajé de la montaña
y fuí buscándome a la reina,
ahora ella caminaba,
ya no era blanca ni violenta;

ella se iba, la sonámbula,
abandonando la pradera,
y yo siguiéndola y siguiéndola
por el pastal y la alameda,

cargada así de tantas flores,
con espaldas y mano aéreas,
siempre cortándolas del aire
y con los aires como siega...

I approached the mountain
now black as Medea,
with not a crevice of brightness,
vague and clear as a cavern.

Those flowers did not grow on branches
or open among rocks.
I cut them from the soft air;
I cut them with gentle shears.

I cut as if I the cutter
walked blind.
I cut from one air and another
as if air were my forest.

When I came down from the mountain
and went in search of my queen,
I found her now walking,
no longer white or violent red.

Somnambulant, she was leaving,
abandoning the meadow,
and I followed her, following
through pastures and poplar groves.

Burdened thus with so many flowers,
shoulders, hands, garlanded with air,
from the air ever cutting more flowers,
I went reaping a harvest of air.

III

Ella delante va sin cara;
ella delante va sin huella,
y yo la sigo todavía
entre los gajos de la niebla,

con estas flores sin color,
ni blanquecinas ni bermejas,
hasta mi entrega sobre el límite,
cuando mi Tiempo se disuelva...

She goes before me, faceless,
leaving no footprint,
and I follow her, still follow
through dense clusters of fog,

bearing colorless flowers,
not white or burnished red,
until my release at the farthest limit
when my time dissolves . . .

La Flor del Aire

y yo la sigo todavía
entre los gajos de la niebla

The Flower of Air

and I follow her, still follow
through dense clusters of fog

La Copa

Yo he llevado una copa
de una isla a otra isla sin despertar el agua.
Si la vertía, una sed traicionaba;
por una gota, el don era caduco;
perdida toda, el dueño lloraría.

No saludé las ciudades;
no dije elogio a su vuelo de torres,
no abrí los brazos en la gran Pirámide
ni fundé casa con corro de hijos.

Pero entregando la copa, yo dije
con el sol nuevo sobre mi garganta:
"Mis brazos ya son libres como nubes sin dueño
y mi cuello se mece en la colina,
de la invitación de los valles."

Mentira fué mi aleluya: miradme.
Yo tengo la vista caída a mis palmas;
camino lenta, sin diamante de agua;
callada voy, y no llevo tesoro,
y me tumba en el pecho y los pulsos
la sangre batida de angustia y de miedo!

The Goblet

I have carried a goblet from one island
to another and never waked its gift of water.
If I had spilled it, I would have betrayed a thirst;
one drop lost, its boon destroyed;
all lost, its owner would have wept.

I did not pause to greet cities
or stay to praise their flight of towers.
I did not fling my arms wide before the great pyramid.
I did not establish a home and a circle of sons.

Delivering the goblet, the new sun
on my throat, I said:
"My arms are now free as vagrant clouds,
and I loll on crests of the hills,
rocked with allure of valleys below."

It was a lie, my alleluia. Look at me.
My eyes are lowered to empty hands.
I walk slowly, without my diamond of water.
I go in silence. I carry no treasure.
And in my breast and through my veins
falls my blood, struck with anguish and fear.

Lagar WINE PRESS 1954

Speech is our second possession, after the soul—and perhaps we have no other possession in this world.

Gabriela was faithful to this concept of the word as a divine gift, and she used it profoundly and conscientiously. She wrote of the stars, the rainbow, clouds and the sky, but she never lost sight of the earth and its people—the man who tills the soil and plants the seed, the miner who works in the cold tomb of the earth so that others can have heat, the child who cries with hunger and the mother who weeps because she cannot feed him. For the people who had no voice, Gabriela became their voice. And for those who could no longer see themselves or their fellow men, who were blind with egotism, envy, hypocrisy, and greed, Gabriela became their eyes and tried to make them see.

Gabriela's friend Palma Guillen de Nicolau says that one of the reasons for the immense popularity of her work was that in both prose and poetry she so often wrote out of the necessity of the moment; her work was "nourished by and constructed from the sap and blood of life. Attentive to the appeal of all who suffer pain, quick to defend all who suffer injustice, Gabriela belonged to those humanists who regard literature as a service."

Many of the poems of *Lagar* (*Wine Press*) are of this nature. Gabriela cried out against persecution, tyranny, racial hatred, war, genocide—crimes perpetrated by man against his brother. She often said, "Of the enemies of the soul—the world, the devil, the flesh— the *world* is the most serious and most dangerous." Gabriela felt that Latin America should try "to create a humanism more Greek than Roman, and saturated with authentic Christianity." Asked what should be the intellectual's response to the political act that cuts off the rights of the individual, she answered: "To resist, to protest, a thousand times *to resist*. It astonishes me to see that the so-called intelligentsia is softened and corrupted by power and money."

Gabriela was above all a whole person, and an integrating force who brought unity out of seemingly disparate things. This self-educated teacher from a remote mountain village, daughter of ancient races—Basque, Incan, Spanish, and (as she liked to claim) Judaic—was a woman whose great capacity for love made her a devout Christian and a member of the Third Order of Saint Francis; whose intellect made her a follower of the disciplines of Buddha; and whose intensity and passion made her a spiritual daughter of King David of Judea. Jorge Mañach has said most aptly, "She was an old voice born anew."

The years during which Gabriela wrote *Lagar* were cruel years. She was not able to "leave behind the dark ravine and climb up gentler slopes" as she had hoped. She encountered the Spanish Civil War and its terrible atrocities; the gathering black clouds of fascism over Europe; and finally the holocaust of World War II. There were deep personal sorrows—the death of many of her close friends, including Stefan Zweig; the death of her sister Emelina; and above all, on a night of horror, the tragic death in Brazil of eighteen-year-old Juan Miguel, affectionately called Yin Yin, whom she had raised and loved as a son. The death of Juan Miguel in 1943 was officially listed as suicide but is believed by many, including myself, to have been a xenophobic and senseless murder. Fierce and bitter poems such as "One Word" ("*Una Palabra*"), the terrible litany of "Mourning" ("*Luto*"), and the prayerful "The Liana" ("*La Liana*") are all expressions of this personal agony of grief.

If these years lived in Europe, Brazil, and finally the United States were filled with tragedy, they also held for Gabriela times of satisfaction and reward. In 1935 Chile passed a law naming her *consul vitalicia*, thus giving her a modest financial security. In 1945, on the initiative of Ecuador, the Latin American Republics unanimously nominated her candidate for the Nobel Prize for Literature; she won this award "for the lyricism fired by powerful sentiment that has made the name of this poet the symbol of idealism in the Latin American world." In 1954, invited by President Carlos Ibañez, Gabriela made her last visit to Chile. Two hundred thousand people gathered before the presidential palace in Santiago to hear her speak. For Gabriela the highlight of this visit was the occasion on which forty-five thousand children, assembled in the national stadium, sang the lyrics of her *Poemas Infantiles*. About a year later, on Human Rights Day, the United Nations invited her to be the sole speaker to address the General Assembly, and Secretary General Dag Hammarskjöld paid honor to her and spoke of the debt all nations owed to her great spirit. Her last public appearance, a few weeks before her death in 1957, was fittingly enough at the Roslyn High School on Long Island, where she gave an informal talk to the American children who were learning Spanish.

In her will she left to the children of Montegrande, her native village, a legacy of her Latin American royalties, and asked to be buried there because she hoped that thus the children of this poor and isolated mountain hamlet might never be forgotten by her country. For all her years of wandering and life in other lands, Gabriela never really left her beloved valley of Elqui and Montegrande where she now rests.

I have all that I lost
and I go carrying my childhood
like a favorite flower
that perfumes my hand.

D.D.

La Otra

Una en mí maté:
yo no la amaba.

Era la flor llameando
del cactus de montaña;
era aridez y fuego;
nunca se refrescaba.

Piedra y cielo tenía
a pies y a espaldas
y no bajaba nunca
a buscar "ojos de agua."

Donde hacía su siesta,
las hierbas se enroscaban
de aliento de su boca
y brasa de su cara.

En rápidas resinas
se endurecía su habla,
por no caer en linda
presa soltada.

Doblarse no sabía
la planta de montaña,
y al costado de ella,
yo me doblaba...

The Other

I killed one of me,
one I did not love.

She was the flame
of mountain cactus.
She was drought and fire,
thirstless.

With rock at her feet
and sky at her shoulder,
she never stooped
in search of cooling springs.

Grass shrivelled
where she rested,
scorched with her breath
and the blazing coal of her face.

Her words hardened
in rapids of resin,
never freed in the spill
of an open dike.

This mountain plant
did not know how to bend.
I bent
at her side.

La dejé que muriese,
robándole mi entraña.
Se acabó como el águila
que no es alimentada.

Sosegó el aletazo,
se dobló, lacia,
y me cayó a la mano
su pavesa acabada ...

Por ella todavía
me gimen sus hermanas,
y las gredas de fuego
al pasar me desgarran.

Cruzando yo les digo:
—Buscad por las quebradas
y haced con las arcillas
otra águila abrasada.

Si no podéis, entonces,
¡ay!, olvidadla.
Yo la maté. ¡Vosotras
también matadla!

I tore my guts from her.
I let her die,
a starving eagle
left unfed.

The thrash of wing grew still.
She toppled, spent,
and fell into my hands,
wasted, consumed.

Her sisters still lament,
accuse me of her death.
The fiery desert chalk
claws as I go by.

Passing, I tell them,
"Search in the cracks of the earth
and mould from its clay
another flaming eagle.

"If you can't, then
forget her.
I killed her. You
kill her, too!"

La Fervorosa

En todos los lugares he encendido
con mi brazo y mi aliento el viejo fuego;
en toda tierra me vieron velando
el faisán que cayó desde los cielos,
y tengo ciencia de hacer la nidada
de las brasas juntando sus polluelos.

Dulce es callando en tendido rescoldo,
tierno cuando en pajuelas lo comienzo.
Malicias sé para soplar sus chispas
hasta que él sube en alocados miembros.
Costó, sin viento, prenderlo, atizarlo:
era o el humo o el chisporroteo;
pero ya sube en cerrada columna
recta, viva, leal y en gran silencio.

No hay gacela que salte los torrentes
y el carrascal como mi loco ciervo;
en redes, peces de oro no brincaron
con rojez de cardumen tan violento.
He cantado y bailado en torno suyo
con reyes, versolaris y cabreros,
y cuando en sus pavesas él moría
yo le supe arrojar mi propio cuerpo.

The Fervent Woman

Everywhere I go, with my arm and my breath
I have kindled the ancient fire.
Everywhere men have seen me
nursing the pheasant fallen from the sky.
I know ways to make a nest of coals,
gathering goslings from the ashes.

Fire is gentle, hushed among spread cinders,
tender when I light it in small straw.
I know tricks to flame its sparks
until it leaps up in crazy limbs.
It took labor to kindle it, raise it in windless air.
It was mere smoke or a crackling.
Now, in great silence, it rises,
a closed column, erect, living, steadfast

No deer leaps over torrents
or through evergreen oaks as swift as my crazy deer.
Golden fish in nets do not thrash
with the redness of such a violent shoal.
I have sung songs and danced around it
with kings, poets, goatherds.
When it died among its ashes
I rekindled it with my own flesh.

Cruzarían los hombres con antorchas
mi aldea, cuando fué mi nacimiento
o mi madre se iría por las cuestas
encendiendo las matas por el cuello.
Espino, algarrobillo y zarza negra,
sobre mi único Valle[1] están ardiendo,
soltando sus torcidas salamandras,
aventando fragancias cerro a cerro.

Mi vieja antorcha, mi jadeada antorcha
va despertando majadas y oteros;
a nadie ciega y va dejando atrás
la noche abierta a rasgones bermejos.
La gracia pido de matarla antes
de que ella mate el Arcángel[2] que llevo.

(Yo no sé si lo llevo o si él me lleva;
pero sé que me llamo su alimento,
y me sé que le sirvo y no le falto
y no lo doy a los titiriteros.)

Corro, echando a la hoguera cuanto es mío.
Porque todo lo di, ya nada llevo,
y caigo yo, pero él no me agoniza
y sé que hasta sin brazos lo sostengo.
O me lo salva alguno de los míos,
hostigando a la noche y su esperpento,
hasta el último hondón, para quemarla
en su cogollo más alto y señero.

[1] Su querido valle de Elqui.
[2] *Arcángel*: antorcha

Men must have passed through my village
with fiery torches the night I was born,
or my mother roamed over the slopes
setting aflame twig-tips of brushwood.
Thorn bush, carob tree, black bramble
are ablaze through my only valley,[1]
throwing off twisted salamanders,
blowing winds of fragrance from hill to hill.

My ancient torch, my panting torch
wakes sheepcotes and hills,
blinds no one, leaves night behind
shred to burnished tatters—
night that I ask the grace to kill, lest she kill
the flaming Archangel[2] I carry.

(I don't know if I carry it, or it carries me,
but I know that I am its very food.
I know that unfailingly I tend it
and never pass it to puppeteers.)

I run, throwing to the fire all that is mine.
I give it all. I carry nothing.
I fall, and falling, its flame is not extinguished.
Should I run armless, I would sustain it,
or one of my kin would save it,
scourging night and her horrors
to the farthest depths,
to set it burning on the highest solitary summit.

[1] Her beloved valley of Elqui.
[2] *Archangel*: torch.

Traje la llama desde la otra orilla,
de donde vine y adonde me vuelvo.
Allá nadie la atiza y ella crece
y va volando en albatrós bermejo.
He de volver a mi hornaza dejando
caer en su regazo el santo préstamo.

¡Padre, madre y hermana adelantados,
y mi Dios vivo que guarda a mis muertos:
corriendo voy por la canal abierta
de vuestra santa Maratón de fuego!

I carry this torch from another shore
from whence I come and to which I return.
There no one stirs the flame that flares and soars
like a fiery albatross.
I shall return to that fire
and let fall there this sacred trust.

Father, mother, and sister who go ahead!
My living God who cares for my dead!
Behold me! I run the open course
of your sacred Marathon of fire!

Emigrada Judía

Voy más lejos que el viento oeste
y el petrel de tempestad.
Paro, interrogo, camino
¡y no duermo por caminar!
Me rebanaron la Tierra,
sólo me han dejado el mar.

Se quedaron en la aldea
casa, costumbre, y dios lar.
Pasan tilos, carrizales
y el Rin que me enseñó a hablar.
No llevo al pecho las mentas
cuyo olor me haga llorar.
Tan sólo llevo mi aliento
y mi sangre y mi ansiedad.

Una soy a mis espaldas,
otra volteada al mar:
mi nuca hierve de adioses,
y mi pecho de ansiedad.

Ya el torrente de mi aldea
no da mi nombre al rodar
y en mi tierra y aire me borro
come huella en arenal.

The Immigrant Jew

I go farther than the west wind,
farther than the stormy petrel I fly.
I stop, I ask, I walk—
never sleep for walking.
A woman cut off from the earth,
they left me only the sea.

Home and habits and household gods
stayed behind in my village
with linden trees and banks of reed grass
on the Rhine that taught me to speak.
I do not bring the mint
whose scent would make me weep.
I bring only my breath,
my blood, my anxiety.

I am two. One looks back,
the other turns to the sea.
The nape of my neck seethes with good-byes
and my breast with yearning.

The stream that flows through my village
no longer speaks my name;
I am erased from my own land and air
like a footprint on the sand.

A cada trecho de ruta
voy perdiendo mi caudal:
una oleada de resinas,
una torre, un robledal.
Suelta mi mano sus gestos
de hacer la sidra y el pan
¡y aventada mi memoria
llegaré desnuda al mar!

With each stretch of road
all that was mine recedes,
a gush of resin, a tower,
a grove of oak trees.
My hands forget their ways
of making cider and bread.
With memory blown clean by the wind,
I arrive naked at the sea.

La Granjera

Para nadie planta la lila
o poda las azaleas
y carga el agua para nadie
en baldes que la espejean.

Vuelta a uno que no da sombra
y sobrepasa su cabeza,
estira un helecho mojado
y a darlo y a hurtárselo juega.

Abre las rejas sin que llamen,
sin que entre nadie, las cierra
y se cansa para el sueño
que la toma, la suelta y la deja.

Desvíen el agua de la vertiente
que la halla gateando ciega,
espolvoreen sal donde siembre,
entierren sus herramientas.

Háganla dormir, pónganla a dormir
como al armiño o la civeta.
Cuando duerma bajen su brazo
y avienten el sueño que sueña.

La muerte anda desvariada,
borracha camina la Tierra,
trueca rutas, tuerce dichas,
en la esfera tamborilea.

The Woman Granger

She plants lilac for no one,
for no one she prunes azaleas;
she carries water for no one
in mirroring pails.

She turns toward one who gives no shadow
and is above her head;
she stretches up a damp fern
and plays at giving and taking.

No one calls and she opens the gates,
she closes them though no one enters.
She grows weary longing for sleep
that takes her, then drops her and leaves her.

Divert the waters of springs
that find her blindly crawling.
Sprinkle salt where she sows,
bury her spade and her hoe.

Make her sleep. Put her to sleep
like an ermine or a civet.
When she sleeps, lower her arm
and throw to the wind the dream she dreams.

For Death walks delirious,
weaves drunken over the earth,
mixes up roads, twists fates,
beats drumbeats on the globe.

Viento y Arcángel[1] de su nombre
trajeron hasta su puerta
la muerte de todos sus vivos
sin traer la muerte de ella.

Las fichas vivas de los hombres
en la carrera le tintinean.
¡Trocaría, perdería
la pobre muerte de la granjera!

[1] El viento Mistral de la Provenza y el Arcángel Gabriel.

The Wind and Archangel[1] whose name she bears
brought to her door
the death of all her living
and never brought hers.

The lively chips of men's fate
jingle as Death runs.
Perhaps he exchanged, perhaps he lost
the poor death of the woman granger.

[1] The Mistral wind of Provence and the Archangel Gabriel.

Ocho Perritos

Los perrillos abrieron sus ojos
del treceavo al quinceavo día.
De golpe vieron el mundo,
con ansia, susto y alegría.
Vieron el vientre de la madre,
la puerta suya que es la mía,
el diluvio de la luz,
las azaleas floridas.

Vieron más: se vieron todos,
el rojo, el negro, el ceniza,
gateando y aupándose,
más vivos que las ardillas;
vieron los ojos de la madre
y mi grito rasgado, y mi risa.

Y yo querría nacer con ellos.
¿Por qué otra vez no sería?
Saltar de unos bananales
una mañana de maravilla,
en can, en coyota, en venada;
mirar con grandes pupilas,
correr, parar, correr, tumbarme
y gemir y saltar de alegría,
acribillada de sol y ladridos
hija de Dios, sierva oscura y divina.

Eight Puppies

Between the thirteenth and the fifteenth day
the puppies opened their eyes.
Suddenly they saw the world,
anxious with terror and joy.
They saw the belly of their mother,
saw the door of their house,
saw a deluge of light,
saw flowering azaleas.

They saw more, they saw all,
the red, the black, the ash.
Scrambling up, pawing and clawing
more lively than squirrels,
they saw the eyes of their mother,
heard my rasping cry and my laugh.

And I wished I were born with them.
Could it not be so another time?
To leap from a clump of banana plants
one morning of wonders—
a dog, a coyote, a deer;
to gaze with wide pupils,
to run, to stop, to run, to fall,
to whimper and whine and jump with joy,
riddled with sun and with barking,
a hallowed child of God, his secret, divine servant.

Despedida de Viajero

La misma ola vagabunda
que te lleva te devuelva.
La ruta no se te enrosque
al cuello como serpiente;
te cargue, te lleve y al fin te deje.

Los que te crucen y miren
de tí se alegren como de fiesta.
Pero que no te retengan
tras de muros y cerrojos
la falsa madre, el falso hijo.

Guarda el repunte del acento,
cela tu risa, cuida tu llanto.
El sol no te curta la frente;
la venteada no te enronquezca
y las ferias y los trueques
no te cierren la mano abierta.

Nadie te dijo de irte.
La tornada no te empuja.
El banco de peces hierve
llamando a sus pescadores.

En la mesa te tuvimos
como alto jarro de plata.
En el fogón escuchándote
te dijimos "pecho de horno."

Farewell to a Traveler

May the same vagabond wave
that takes you, return you.
May the road not entwine itself
about your neck like a serpent.
May it take you and carry you, but at last leave you.

May those on your path who see you
take joy of you as of a festival.
But don't be retained
behind walls or bolts
by a false mother, a false son.

Guard against the rise of foreign accents;
defend your laughter, your cry.
May the sun not weather your forehead
or exposure hoarsen your voice,
or tricks of carnival or commerce
close your open hand.

No one told you to go.
No one hastens your return.
But shoals of fish teem,
calling to their fishermen.

We had you at our table
like a tall silver pitcher.
Listening to you by the fireside
we called you "breast of oven."

Bajo palmera o tamarindo,
despierto o dormido, entero o roto,
Rafael Arcángel vaya a tu lado
y tu Isla de palmeras
raye tus ropas, bese tu cara.

Enderézate entonces y salta
como el delfín a las olas.
El rumbo Este como el tábano
te punce, te hostigue y te venza.

Vuelve, hijo, por nosotros
que somos piedras de umbrales
y no barqueros ni calafates
desde que rompimos los remos
y que enterramos las barcas.

En la costa, curvados de noche,
te encenderemos fogatas
por si olvidaste la ensenada.
Te pondrá en la arena la marea
como a alga o como a niño
y todos te gritaremos
por albricias, por albricias.

En corro, en anillo, en nudo,
riendo y llorando enseñaremos
al trascordado a hablar de nuevo
cuando te broten y rebroten
tus gestos en el semblante,
nuestros nombres en tu boca.

Beneath palm trees or tamarinth,
waking or sleeping, whole or broken,
may the Archangel Raphael go by your side,
may your island of palm trees cast fronded shadows
on your clothing, and kiss your face.

Rise then, and leap
like a dolphin to the waves.
May the way home, like a gadfly,
sting you, goad you, and conquer.

Come back, son, for our sake,
we who are stones of thresholds,
and never again boatsmen or calkers
since we broke our oars
and buried our boats.

On the coast, our backs curved to the night,
we will light fires for you
should you forget the bay.
The tide will set you on the sand
like an alga or a child
and we will all cry aloud
for joy, for joy.

In a round, in a ring, in a knot,
laughing and crying, we will teach
our forgetful one to speak again
when your old expression breaks forth on your face
and our names burst again from your mouth.

Una Piadosa

Quiero ver al hombre del faro,
quiero ir a la peña del risco,
probar en su boca la ola,
ver en sus ojos el abismo.
Yo quiero alcanzar, si vive,
al viejo salobre y salino.

Dicen que sólo mira al Este,
—emparedado que está vivo—
y quiero, cortando sus olas
que me mire en vez del abismo.

Todo se sabe de la noche
que ahora es mi lecho y camino:
sabe resacas, pulpos, esponjas,
sabe un grito que mata el sentido.

Está escupido de marea
su pecho fiel y con castigo,
está silbado de gaviotas
y tan albo como el herido
¡y de inmóvil, y mudo y ausente,
ya no parece ni nacido!

Pero voy a la torre del faro,
subiéndome ruta de filos
por el hombre que va a contarme
lo terrestre y lo divino,
y en brazo y brazo le llevo
jarro de leche, sorbo de vino...

A Pious One

I must see the lighthouse keeper,
go to his craggy rock,
feel the wave break in his mouth,
see the abyss in his eyes.
I want to find him, if he lives,
that old salt man of sea.

They say he looks only eastward,
walled-up alive at sea.
When I shatter his wave, I wish
he would turn his eyes from the abyss to me.

He knows all there is to know of night
which has become my bed and path;
he knows the octopus, sponge, and undertow,
and the senses slain by a scream.

His chastened breast
is spat upon by tides,
is shrilled by gulls,
is white as the maimed.
So still, so mute and unmindful
as though unborn.

But I go to the lighthouse tower
to climb the knife-edged path
and be with the man who will tell me
what is earthly and what divine.
In one arm I bring him a jug of milk,
in the other, a sip of wine.

Y él sigue escuchando mares
que no aman sino a sí mismos.
Pero tal vez ya nada escuche,
de haber parado en sal y olvido.

On he goes listening to seas
in love with nothing but themselves.
Perhaps now he listens to nothing,
fixed in forgetfulness and salt.

Mujer de Prisionero

Yo tengo en esa hoguera de ladrillos,
yo tengo al hombre mío prisionero.
Por corredores de filos amargos
y en esta luz sesgada de murciélago,
tanteando como el buzo por la gruta,
voy caminando hasta que me lo encuentro,
y hallo a mi cebra pintada de burla
en los anillos de su befa envuelto.

Me lo han dejado, como a barco roto,
con anclas de metal en los pies tiernos;
le han esquilado como a la vicuña
su gloria azafranada de cabellos.
Pero su Angel-Custodio anda la celda
y si nunca lo ven es que están ciegos.
Entró con él al hoyo de cisterna;
tomó los grillos como obedeciendo;
se alzó a coger el vestido de cobra,
y se quedó sin el aire del cielo.

El Angel gira moliendo y moliendo
la harina densa del más denso sueño;
le borra el mar de zarcos oleajes,
le sumerge una casa y un viñedo,
y le esconde mi ardor de carne en llamas,
y su esencia, y el nombre que dieron.

The Prisoner's Wife

In this blazing bonfire of brick
they keep my love, my husband, prisoner.
Through corridors of bitter, knife-sharp edges,
in this oblique bat-gloom of light,
groping like a sea-diver through grottos,
I walk—I walk until I find him
ringed with scoffing stripes,
my love, a zebra, painted in mockery.

They have left him for me like a shattered boat
with iron anchors on his tender feet.
They have sheared him like a vicuna,
stripped the saffron glory of his hair.
But his guardian angel walks his cell—
if they do not see him they are blind.
His angel entered with him this cistern pit,
took on sham fetters of obedience,
stood up to receive the cobra shirt
and remained, cut off from air and sky.

His angel mills and grinds
the dense flour of deepest sleep.
He wipes out a sea of pale blue water,
submerges a house, engulfs a vineyard,
hides from him the ardor of my flesh aflame,
hides his essence and his very name.

En la celda, las olas de bochorno
y frío, de los dos, yo me las siento,
y trueque y turno que hacen y deshacen
de queja y queja los dos prisioneros
¡y su guardián nocturno ni ve ni oye
que dos espaldas son y dos lamentos!

Al rematar el pobre día nuestro,
hace el Angel dormir al prisionero,
dando y lloviendo olvido imponderable
a puñados de noche y de silencio.
Y yo desde mi casa que lo gime
hasta la suya, que es dedal ardiendo,
como quien no conoce otro camino,
en lanzadera viva voy y vengo,
y al fin se abren los muros y me dejan
pasar el hierro, la brea, el cemento...

En lo oscuro, mi amor que come moho
y telarañas, cuando es que yo llego,
entero ríe a lo blanquidorado;
a mi piel, a mi fruta y a mi cesto.
El canasto de frutas a hurtadillas
destapo, y uva a uva se lo entrego;
la sidra se la doy pausadamente,
porque el sorbo no mate a mi sediento,
y al moverse le siguen—pajarillos
de perdición—sus grillos cenicientos.

Every wave of heat scorching their cell,
every icy gust, blows through me.
I feel every twist and turn made
by the suffering of *two* prisoners.
But the night guard does not see two backs,
does not hear two laments.

When our wretched day ends, his angel
lets sleep fall upon the prisoner,
rains imponderable oblivion
in fistfuls of night and silence.
From the house where I grieve
to the fiery thimble of his dungeon,
I fly back and forth like a living shuttle,
like one who knows no other path,
until at last the walls open and let me pass
through iron, pitch, and mortar . . .

My love who eats mold and cobwebs in the dark,
breaks into crazy laughter when I come,
laughs at the golden-white of my skin,
laughs at the basket and fruit I bring.
Stealthily I open the hamper of fruit
and feed him grapes, one by one;
pour him cider, sip by sip,
lest drinking kill my thirsty lover.
When he moves, ashen chains follow—
birds of perdition, vultures.

Vuestro hermano vivía con vosotros
hasta el día de cielo y umbral negro;
pero es hermano vuestro, mientras sea
la sal aguda y el agraz acedo,
hermano con su cifra y sin su cifra,
y libre o tanteando en su agujero,
y es bueno, sí, que hablemos de él, sentados
o caminando, y en vela o durmiendo,
si lo hemos de contar como una fábula
cuando nos haga responder su Dueño.

Cuando rueda la nieve los tejados
o a sus espaldas cae el aguacero,
mi calor con su hielo se pelea
en el pecho de mi hombre friolento:
él ríe, ríe a mi nombre y mi rostro
y al cesto ardiendo con que lo festejo,
¡y puedo, calentando sus rodillas,
contar como David todos sus huesos![1]

[1] Salmo XXII, versos 16–18:
  "Porque perros me han rodeado,
  Hame cercado cuadrilla de malignos:
  Horadaron mis manos y mis pies.
  Contar puedo todos mis huesos;
  Ellos miran, considéranme.
  Partieron entre sí mis vestidos,
  Y sobre mi ropa echaron suertes."

He is your brother. He lived with you
until the day of black threshold and sky.
He is your brother as long as
salt is sharp and verjuice sour.
He is your brother, wearing a number or without a number,
walking free or groping in his cell.
It is good that we talk of him,
resting or walking, wakeful or sleeping,
since we must account for him
when his Lord calls us to answer.

When snowfall whirls on the rooftops,
when cloudburst breaks on his shoulder,
my warmth wrestles with his dank cold
in the breast of my shivering love.
He laughs, laughs at my name and my face,
at the flaming basket I bring for his feast;
and warming his knees like King David
I may tell his every bone.[1]

[1] Psalm XXII, verses 16–18:
  "For dogs have compassed me:
  the assembly of the wicked have inclosed me:
  they pierced my hands and my feet.
  I may tell all my bones;
  they look and stare upon me.
  They part my garments among them,
  and cast lots upon my vesture."

Pero por más que le allegue mi hálito
y le funda su sangre pecho a pecho,
¡cómo con brazo arqueado de cuna
yo rompo cedro y pizarra de techos,
si en dos mil días los hombres sellaron
este panal cuya cera de infierno
más arde más, que aceites y resinas,
y que la pez, y arde mudo y sin tiempo!

However close my breath on him,
melting his blood, my breast on his,
still—how can this arm that curves like a cradle
ever smash cedar and slate of rooftops
when men have sealed off for two thousand days
this hellish honeycomb whose wax
burns more fiery than oil or resin
or pitch—burns mute and timeless!

Tiempo

AMANECER

Hincho mi corazón para que entre
como cascada ardiente el Universo.
El nuevo día llega y su llegada
me deja sin aliento.
Canto como la gruta que es colmada
canto mi día nuevo.

Por la gracia perdida y recobrada
humilde soy sin dar y recibiendo
hasta que la Gorgona de la noche
va, derrotada, huyendo.

Time

DAYBREAK

My heart swells that the Universe
like a fiery cascade may enter.
The new day comes. Its coming
leaves me breathless.
I sing. Like a cavern brimming
I sing my new day.

For grace lost and recovered
I stand humble. Not giving. Receiving.
Until the Gorgon night,
vanquished, flees.

MAÑANA

Es ella devuelta, es ella devuelta.
Cada mañana la misma y otra.
Que lo esperado ayer y siempre
ha de llegar esta mañana.

Mañanas de manos vacías,
que prometieron y defraudaron.
Mirar abrirse otra mañana
saltar como el ciervo del Este
despierta, feliz y nueva,
vívida, alácrita y rica de obras.

Alce el hermano la cabeza
caída al pecho y recíbala.
Sea digno de la que salta
y como alción se lanza y sube,
alción dorado que baja cantando
¡Aleluya, aleluya, aleluya!

MORNING

She has returned! She has returned!
Each morning the same and new.
Awaited every yesterday,
she must return this morning.

Mornings of empty hands
that promised and betrayed.
Behold this new morning unfold,
leap like a deer from the East,
awake, happy and new,
alert, eager and rich with deeds.

Brother, raise up your head
fallen to your breast. Receive her.
Be worthy of her who leaps up,
soars and darts like a halcyon,
golden halcyon plunging earthward singing
Alleluia, alleluia, alleluia!

ATARDECER

Siento mi corazón en la dulzura
fundirse como ceras:
son un óleo tardo
y no un vino mis venas,
y siento que mi vida se va huyendo
callada y dulce como la gacela.

AFTERNOON

I feel my heart melt like wax
in this sweetness:
slow oil, not wine,
my veins,
I feel my life fleeting
silent and sweet as a gazelle.

NOCHE

Las montañas se deshacen,
el ganado se ha perdido;
el sol regresa a su fragua:
todo el mundo se va huido.

Se va borrando la huerta,
la granja se ha sumergido
y mi cordillera sume
su cumbre y su grito vivo.

Las criaturas resbalan
de soslayo hacia el olvido,
y también los dos rodamos
hacia la noche, mi niño.

NIGHT

Mountain ranges dissolve,
cattle wander astray,
the sun returns to its forge,
all the world slips away.

Orchard and garden are fading,
the farmhouse already immersed.
My mountains submerge their crests
and their living cry.

All creatures are sliding aslant
down toward forgetfulness and sleep.
You and I, also, my baby,
tumble down toward night's keep.

Amanecer

El nuevo día llega y su llegada
me deja sin aliento

Daybreak

The new day comes. Its coming
leaves me breathless

Una Palabra[1]

Yo tengo una palabra en la garganta
y no la suelto, y no me libro de ella
aunque me empuje su empellón de sangre.
Si la soltase, quema el pasto vivo,
sangra al cordero, hace caer al pájaro.

Tengo que desprenderla de mi lengua,
hallar un agujero de castores
o sepultarla con cales y cales
porque no guarde como el alma el vuelo.

No quiero dar señales de que vivo
mientras que por mi sangre vaya y venga
y suba y baje por mi loco aliento.
Aunque mi padre Job la dijo, ardiendo,
no quiero darle, no, mi pobre boca
porque no ruede y la hallen las mujeres
que van al río, y se enrede a sus trenzas
o al pobre matorral tuerza y abrase.

Yo quiero echarle violentas semillas
que en una noche la cubran y ahoguen
sin dejar de ella el cisco de una sílaba.
O rompérmela así, como a la víbora
que por mitad se parte con los dientes.

[1] Se trata de la muerte de Yin Yin.

One Word[1]

I have in my throat one word
that I cannot speak, will not free
though its thrust of blood pounds me.
If I voiced it, it would scorch the living grass,
bleed the lamb, fell the bird.

I have to cut it from my tongue,
find a beaver's hole,
or bury it beneath lime and more quicklime
lest, soul-like, it break free.

I wish to give no sign of what I live
as this word courses through my blood, ebbs and flows,
rises, falls with each mad breath.
Though Job, my father, burning, spoke it,
I will not give it utterance
lest it roll vagrant
and be found by river-women,
twist itself in their braids,
or mangle and blaze the poor thicket.

I wish to throw seeds so violent
they burst and smother it in one night
leaving not even a syllable's trace.
Or rip it from myself
with the serpent's severing tooth.

[1] This poem deals with the death of Yin Yin.

Y volver a mi casa, entrar, dormirme,
cortada de ella, rebanada de ella,
y despertar después de dos mil días
recién nacida de sueño y olvido.

¡Sin saber más que tuve una palabra
de yodo y piedra-alumbre entre los labios
ni saber acordarme de una noche,
de una morada en país extranjero,
de la celada y el rayo a la puerta
y de mi carne marchando sin su alma!

And return to my house, enter and sleep,
torn from it, sliced from it;
wake after two thousand days
newly born out of sleep and oblivion.

Never again to remember the word between my lips,
that word of iodine and alum stone,
or ever again that one night,
the ambush in a foreign land,
the lightning bolt at the door
and my flesh abroad with no soul.

Hospital

Detrás del muro encalado
que no deja pasar el soplo
y me ciega de su blancura,
arden fiebres que nunca toco,
brazos perdidos caen manando,
ojos marinos miran, ansiosos.

En sus lechos penan los hombres,
metales blancos bajo su forro,
y cada uno dice lo mismo
que yo, en la vaina de su sollozo.

Uno se muere con su mensaje
en el desuello del fruto mondo,
y mi oído iba a escucharlo
toda la noche, rostro con rostro.

Hacia el cristal de mi desvelo,
adonde baja lo que ignoro,
caen dorsos que no sujeto,
rollos de partos que no recojo,
y vienen carnes estrujadas
de lagares que no conozco.

Juntos estamos, según las cañas,
oyéndonos como los chopos,
y más distantes que Gea y Sirio,
y el pobre coipo del faisán rojo.
Porque yo tengo y ellos tienen
muro yerto que vuelve el torso,
y no deja acudir los brazos,
ni se abre al amor deseoso.

Hospital

Behind the whitewashed wall
which no breath enters,
whose whiteness blinds me,
burn fevers I never touch,
lost arms fall as they reach up,
sea-blue eyes look out fearfully.

Men in pain lie on their beds—
white metals under covers—
and each one says the same as I
in the sheath of his sob.

One dies, his message lost
in the neat paring of a fruit.
I was ready to listen to it
all night long, my head against his.

Into the core of my wakefulness
falls all I do not know,
bodies I cannot support,
bundles of birth I cannot pick up,
flesh squeezed from wine presses
unknown.

We are together like sugar cane,
poplars listening in a grove—
more distant than beaver and pheasant,
than Gea and Sirius.
Between us stands
this unyielding wall, back turned,
shutting out helping arms,
blind to longing love.

El Celador costado blanco
nunca se parte en grietas de olmo,
y aunque me cele como un hijo
no me consiente ir a los otros:
espalda lisa que me guarda
sin volteadura y sin escorzo.

El Sordo quiere que vivamos
todos perdidos, juntos y solos,
sabiéndonos y en nuestra búsqueda,
en laberinto blanco y redondo,
hoy al igual de ayer, lo mismo
que en un cuento de hombre beodo,
aunque suban, del otro canto
de la noche, cuellos ansiosos,
y me nombren la Desvariada,
el que hace señas y el Niño loco.

This white-flanked warden,
impregnable,
watches over me like a son,
yet keeps me from the others;
it guards me, a smooth back
implacable and unrelenting.

The deaf one wills that we live lost,
together and alone,
knowing each other, circling
in our search through the white labyrinth—
today the same as yesterday
as in a drunkard's tale,
though necks crane anxiously
from the other side of night
while *the man-who-makes-signals*
and *the mad child*
call me *the crazy one*.

Una Mujer

Donde estaba su casa sigue
como si no hubiera ardido.
Habla sólo la lengua de su alma
con los que cruzan, ninguna.

Cuando dice "pino de Alepo"
no dice árbol que dice un niño
y cuando dice "regato"
y "espejo de oro,"[1] dice lo mismo.

Cuando llega la noche cuenta
los tizones de su casa
o enderezada su frente
ve erguido su pino de Alepo.
(El día vive por su noche
y la noche por su milagro.)

En cada árbol endereza
al que acostaron en tierra
y en el fuego de su pecho
lo calienta, lo enrolla, lo estrecha.

[1] Apodos de cariño que Gabriela solía poner a Yin Yin.

A Woman

Where her house stood, she goes on living
as if it had never burned.
The only words she speaks
are the words of her soul;
to those who pass by she speaks none.

When she says "pine of Aleppo"
she speaks of no tree, but a child;
and when she says "little stream"
or "mirror of gold"[1] she speaks of the same.

When night falls she counts
the charred beams of her house.
Lifting her forehead she sees
the pine of Aleppo stand tall.
(The day lives for its night,
the night for its miracle.)

In every tree, she raises the one
they laid upon the earth.
She warms and wraps and holds him close
to the fire of her breast.

[1] Gabriela's affectionate nicknames for Yin Yin.

La Liana

En el secreto de la noche
mi oración sube como las lianas,
así cayendo y levantando
y a tanteos como el ciego,
pero viendo más que el buho.

Por el tallo de la noche
que tu amabas y que yo amo,
ella sube despedazada
y rehecha, insegura y cierta.

Aquí la rompe una derrota
más allá un aire la endereza.
Una camada de aire la aúpa
un no sé qué me la derriba.

O ya trepa como la liana
y el geiser a cada salto
recibidos y devueltos.

O ella es y yo no soy;
ella crece y yo perezco.
Pero yo tengo mi duro aliento
y mi razón y mi locura,
y la retengo y la rehago
al pie del tallo de la noche.

The Liana

In the secret of night
my prayer climbs like the liana,
gropes like a blind man,
sees more than the owl.

Up the stalk of night
that you loved, that I love,
creeps my torn prayer,
rent and mended, uncertain and sure.

Here the path breaks it,
here breezes lift it,
wind flurries toss it,
and something I don't know
hurls it to earth again.

Now it creeps like the liana,
now geysers up, at every thrust
received and returned.

My prayer is, and I am not.
It grows, and I perish.
I have only my hard breath,
my reason and my madness.
I cling to the vine of my prayer.
I tend it at the root
of the stalk of night.

Y es siempre la misma gloria
de vida y la misma muerte:
tú que me ves y yo que te oigo,
y la pobre liana que sube
y cayendo remece mi cuerpo.

Coge el cabo desfallecido
de mi oración, cuando te alcanza,
para saber que la tomaste
y la sostengas la noche entera.

La noche se hace de pronto dura
como el ipé y el eucalipto;
se vuelve cinta de camino
o queda y dura en río helado.
¡Y mi liana sube y te alcanza
hasta rasarte los costados!

Cuando se rompe tú me la alzas
con los pulsos que te conozco,
y entonces se doblan mi soplo
mi calentura y mi mensaje.
Sosiego, te nombro, te digo
uno por uno todos los nombres.
¡La liana alcanza a tu cuello
lo rodea, lo anuda y se aplaca!

Se aviva entonces mi pobre soplo
y las palabras se hacen río,
y mi oración así arribada
¡al fin sosiega, al fin descansa!

Always the same glory
of life, the same death,
you who hear me and I who see you,
and the vine that tenses, snaps, recoils,
lacerates my flesh.

Grasp the weakening tip
when my prayer reaches you
so that I may know you have it;
sustain it the long night.

Of an instant night hardens,
hard as ipecac, as eucalyptus:
becomes black stretch of road
and frozen hush of river.
My liana climbs and climbs
till tendrils touch your side.

When the vine breaks, you raise it,
and by your touch I know you.
Then my breath abates,
my ardor and my message.
I grow still. I name you. One by one
I tell you all your names.
The liana caresses your throat,
binds you fast, entwines you, and rests.

My poor breath quickens
and words become flood.
My prayer, moored, at last
grows quiet, at last is still.

Entonces ya sé que arriba
la liana oscura de mi sangre
y el rollo roto de mi cuerpo,
en oración desovillado,
y aprendo yo que la paciente
gime cortada, luego se junta
y vuelve a subir, y subiendo
a más padece, más alcanza.

En esta noche tú recoge
mi llamado, tómalo y ténlo;
duerme, mi amor, y por ella
hazme bajar mi propio sueño,
y como era sobre la tierra,
así amor mío, así quedemos.

Then I know the dark vine
of my blood is anchored,
the broken skein of my body
unraveled in prayer;
and I learn that the patient
cry, broken, mends;
climbs again and climbing,
the more it suffers, the more attains.

Gather up my prayer tonight.
Take it and hold it.
Sleep, my love, let my sleep
fall to me in prayer,
and as we were on earth,
so let us remain.

Marta y María[1]

Nacieron juntas, vivían juntas,
comían juntas Marta y María.
Cerraban las mismas puertas,
al mismo aljibe bebían,
el mismo soto las miraba,
y la misma luz las vestía.

Sonaban las lozas de Marta,
borbolleaban sus marmitas.
El gallinero hervía en tórtolas,
en gallos rojos y ave-frías,
y, saliendo y entrando, Marta
en plumazones se perdía.

Rasgaba el aire, gobernaba
alimentos y lencerías,
el lagar y las colmenas
y el minuto, la hora y el día...

Y a ella todo le voceaba
a grito herido por donde iba:
vajillas, puertas, cerrojos,
como a la oveja con esquila;
y a la otra se le callaban,
hilado llanto y Ave-Marías.

[1] Marta y María eran las hermanas de Lázaro. Se identifica a veces a María con María Magdalena.

Martha and Mary[1]

They were born together, lived together,
ate together—Martha and Mary.
They closed the same door,
drank from the same well,
were watched by one thicket,
clothed by one light.

Martha's cups and dishes clattered,
her kettles bubbled.
Her chickenyard teemed with roosters,
a whirr of plover and dove.
She bustled to and fro
lost in a cloud of feathers.

Martha cut the air, reigned
over meals and linen,
governed wine press and beehives,
ruled the minute, the hour, the day . . .

A wounded outcry sounded
wherever she came and went.
Dishes, doors, bolts clamored
as to a belled sheep.
But all grew hushed when her sister passed by,
thin keening and Hail Marys.

[1] Martha and Mary were the sisters of Lazarus. Mary is sometimes identified with Mary Magdalene.

Mientras que en ángulo encalado,
sin alzar mano, aunque tejía,
María, en azul mayólica,
algo en el aire quieto hacía:
¿Qué era aquello que no se acababa,
ni era mudado ni le cundía?

Y un mediodía ojidorado,
cuando es que Marta rehacía
a diez manos la vieja Judea,
sin voz ni gesto *pasó* María.

Sólo se hizo más dejada,
sólo embebió sus mejillas,
y se quedó en santo y seña
de su espalda, en la cal fría,
un helecho tembloroso,
una lenta estalactita,
y no más que un gran silencio
que rayo ni grito rompían.

Cuando Marta envejeció,
sosegaron horno y cocina;
la casa ganó su sueño,
quedó la escalera² supina,
y en adormeciendo Marta,
y pasando de roja a salina,
fué a sentarse acurrucada
en el ángulo de María,
donde con pasmo y silencio
apenas su boca movía...

² En el campo se usa una escalera de mano para subir al desván.

In a whitewashed corner,
Mary in blue majolica
wove some strange thing in the quiet air
though she never raised her hand.
What was this thing that never finished,
never altered or increased?

One golden-eyed noon
while Martha with ten hands
was busy reshaping old Judea,
without a word or sign, Mary *passed on.*

She merely grew more languid,
her cheeks indrawn;
the mark of her body and spirit
imprinted in the cold lime,
a trembling fern,
a slow stalactite;
no more than a great silence
that no cry or lightning bolt could shatter.

When Martha grew old,
oven and kitchen grew quiet,
the house gained its sleep,
the ladder[2] lay supine;
and falling asleep,
her flesh shrivelling from ruddy to ash,
Martha went to crouch
in Mary's corner
where with wonder and silence
her mouth scarcely moved . . .

2 In rural areas a ladder is used as steps to the sleeping loft.

Hacia María pedía ir
y hacia ella se iba, se iba,
diciendo: "¡María!", sólo eso,
y volviendo a decir: "¡María!"
Y con tanto fervor llamaba
que, sin saberlo, ella partía,
soltando la hebra del hálito
que su pecho no defendía.
Ya iba los aires subiendo,
ya "no era" y no lo sabía ...

She asked to go to Mary
and toward her she went, she went
murmuring, "Mary!"—only that,
repeating, "Mary!"
And she called out with such fervor
that, without knowing, she departed,
letting loose the filament of breath
that her breast did not protect.
Now she left, ascending the air;
now she was no longer and did not know it . . .

La Desasida

En el sueño yo no tenía
padre ni madre, gozos ni duelos,
no era mío ni el tesoro
que he de velar hasta el alba,
edad ni nombre llevaba,
ni mi triunfo ni mi derrota.

Mi enemigo podía injuriarme
o negarme Pedro, mi amigo,
que de haber ido tan lejos
no me alcanzaban las flechas:
para la mujer dormida
lo mismo daba este mundo
que los otros no nacidos...

Donde estuve nada dolía:
estaciones, sol ni lunas,
no punzaban ni la sangre
ni el cardenillo del Tiempo;
ni los altos silos subían
ni rondaba el hambre los silos.
Y yo decía como ebria:
"¡Patria mía, Patria, *la Patria*!"

Pero un hilo tibio retuve,
—pobre mujer—en la boca,
vilano que iba y venía
por la nonada del soplo,
no más que un hilo de araña
o que un repunte de arenas.

The Disburdened

In dream I had no father
or mother, joys or sorrows.
Even the treasure I must guard
until dawn was not mine.
I bore no age or name,
no triumph or defeat.

My enemy could wrong me,
and my friend Peter could deny me.
I had gone so far
that arrows could not reach me.
To a woman sleeping
it is all the same, this world
and the others unborn . . .

Where I was nothing pained.
Neither seasons, sun, nor moons
could nettle the blood
or pierce the verdigris of time.
No tall silos rose,
circled round by hunger.
And as one made drunk, I cried out:
Patria mía, Patria, la Patria!

But—poor woman—there clung
to my mouth one warm thread
that came and went like thistledown
with every nothingness of breath.
It was no more than spider's thread,
thin as the line of ebbing tide.

Pude no volver y he vuelto.
De nuevo hay muro a mi espalda,
y he de oír y responder
y, voceando pregones,
ser otra vez buhonera.

Tengo mi cubo de piedra
y el puñado de herramientas.
Mi voluntad la recojo
como ropa abandonada,
desperezo mi costumbre
y otra vez retomo el mundo.

Pero me iré cualquier día
sin llantos y sin abrazos,
barca que parte de noche
sin que la sigan las otras,
la ojeen los faros rojos
ni se la oigan sus costas . . .

I could have not returned, and I returned.
Now again the wall at my shoulder
and I must hear and give answer,
and with hawker's cry
be once again the peddler.

I have my block of stone
and a handful of tools.
I gather up my will
like abandoned clothes,
I shake familiar habits from their sleep
and once again take up the world.

But one day I shall go
without cries, without embraces,
a ship that leaves by night
that others cannot follow,
not seen by the red eye of beacons,
not heard by the shores.

Puertas

Entre los gestos del mundo
recibí el que dan las puertas.
En la luz yo las he visto
o selladas o entreabiertas
y volviendo sus espaldas
del color de la vulpeja.
¿Por qué fué que las hicimos
para ser sus prisioneras?

Del gran fruto de la casa
son la cáscara avarienta.
El fuego amigo que gozan
a la ruta no lo prestan.
Canto que adentro cantamos
lo sofocan sus maderas
y a su dicha no convidan
como la granada abierta:
¡Sibilas llenas de polvo,
nunca mozas, nacidas viejas!

Parecen tristes moluscos
sin marea y sin arenas.
Parecen, en lo ceñudo,
la nube de la tormenta.
A las sayas verticales
de la Muerte se asemejan
y yo las abro y las paso
como la caña que tiembla.

Doors

Among the gestures the world makes,
I received those made by doors.
I have seen them in full light
closed or ajar,
turning their fox-colored backs.
Why did we create them
to become their prisoners?

The house, a great fruit;
doors, the jealous rind.
They do not lend to the road
the friendly fire they enjoy.
Their wood smothers
the song we sing within.
Unlike the open pomegranate
they never share their joy.
Dusty Sibyls!
Never young, born old!

They sadden like mollusks
without tides or sand,
they glower like clouds
that hold the storm.
They are the vertical
garments of Death.
I open them and pass through them
like a trembling reed.

"¡No!", dicen a las mañanas
aunque las bañen, las tiernas.
Dicen "¡No!" al viento marino
que en su frente palmotea
y al olor de pinos nuevos
que se viene por la Sierra.
Y lo mismo que Casandra,
no salvan aunque bien sepan:
porque mi duro destino
él también pasó mi puerta.

Cuando golpeo me turban
igual que la vez primera.
El seco dintel da luces
como la espada despierta
y los batientes se avivan
en escapadas gacelas.

Entro como quien levanta
paño de cara encubierta,
sin saber lo que me tiene
mi casa de angosta almendra
y pregunto si me aguarda
mi salvación o mi pérdida.

They say "No!" to the mornings
that tenderly bathe them.
They say "No!" to the sea wind
that claps a cool hand to their foreheads.
"No!" to the scent of new pines
that blows down from the hill.
Like Cassandra, they know our fate
and will not save us with their knowledge,
for my cruel destiny
walked through my door.

When I knock, they alarm me
as the first time.
The dry lintel sparks
like a drawn sword,
doors spring to life
like escaping gazelles.

I enter as one who raises
a cloth from a covered face,
not knowing what the narrow
almond husk of my house holds for me—
my salvation or my ruin.

Ya quiero irme y dejar
el sobrehaz de la Tierra,
el horizonte que acaba
como un ciervo, de tristeza,
y las puertas de los hombres
selladas como cisternas.
Por no voltear en la mano
sus llaves de anguilas muertas
y no oírles más el crótalo
que me sigue la carrera.

Voy a cruzar sin gemido
la última vez por ellas
y a alejarme tan gloriosa
como la esclava liberta,
siguiendo el cardumen vivo
de mis muertos que me llevan.
No estarán allá rayados
por cubo y cubo de puertas
ni ofendidos por sus muros
como el herido en sus vendas.

I wish to go, leave behind me
the surface of the earth,
horizons dying
like deer with sadness,
leave behind me doors of men
sealed like cisterns,
never again to turn in my hand
their keys of dead eels,
and never again hear their rattle
follow my fleeing footsteps.

I will pass through them
for the last time without lament.
Jubilant as a freed slave,
I will leave them behind
and follow the living shoal
of my dead that carry me.
My dead will not be imprisoned there
by slabs and slabs of doors,
nor hurt by walls
like the wounded bound in gauze.

Vendrán a mí sin embozo,
oreados de luz eterna.
Cantaremos a mitad
de los cielos y la tierra.
Con el canto apasionado
haremos caer las puertas
y saldrán de ellas los hombres
como niños que despiertan
al oír que se descuajan
y que van cayendo muertas.

They will come to me unveiled
in air and eternal light.
Half-way between heaven and earth
we will burst into song;
we will fell the doors
with the passion of our song.
Hearing their crash
and shuddering fall,
men will come rushing out
like children that awake.

El Reparto

Si me ponen al costado
la ciega de nacimiento,
le diré, bajo, bajito,
con la voz llena de polvo:
—Hermana, toma mis ojos.

¿Ojos? ¿para qué preciso
arriba y llena de lumbres?
En mi Patria he de llevar
todo el cuerpo hecho pupila,
espejo devolvedor
ancha pupila sin párpados.

Iré yo a campo traviesa
con los ojos en las manos
y las dos manos dichosas
deletreando lo no visto
nombrando lo adivinado.

Tome otra mis rodillas
si las suyas se quedaron
trabadas y empedernidas
por las nieves o la escarcha.

Otra tómeme los brazos
si es que se los rebanaron.
Y otras tomen mis sentidos
con su sed and con su hambre.

Distribution

If I am put beside
the born blind,
I will tell her softly, so softly
with my voice of dust,
"Sister, take my eyes."

Eyes? Why do I need them
where all is brightness?
Where I go I must wear a body
that is all eye,
the returning mirror,
the wide pupil with no eyelid.

I will go cross-country
using my hands for eyes,
my hands happy
spelling out the newly seen,
naming by name what is divined.

Let another take my knees
if hers have grown
stiff and unbending
with snow or frost.

Let another take my arms
if hers have been sundered.
And others take my senses
with their thirst and hunger.

Acabe así, consumada
repartida como hogaza
y lanzada a sur o a norte
no seré nunca más una.

Será mi aligeramiento
como un apear de ramas
que me abajan y descargan
de mí misma, como de árbol.

¡Ah, respiro, ay dulce pago,
vertical descendimiento!

Let me finish thus, consumed,
divided like a loaf of bread.
Thrown to the South or to the North,
I shall never again be one.

This dismantling of myself will be
like the pruning of branches
that drop from me and lighten my burden
as with a tree.

Ah! Sweet relief! Sweet expiation!
Vertical descent!

Luto

En sólo una noche brotó de mi pecho,
subió, creció el árbol de luto,
empujó los huesos, abrió las carnes,
su cogollo llegó a mi cabeza.

Sobre hombros, sobre espaldas,
echó hojazones y ramas,
y en tres días estuve cubierta,
rica de él como de mi sangre.
¿Dónde me palpan ahora?
¿Qué brazo daré que no sea luto?

Igual que las humaredas
ya no soy llama ni brasas.
Soy esta espiral y esta liana
y este ruedo de humo denso.

Todavía los que llegan
me dicen mi nombre, me ven la cara;
pero yo que me ahogo me veo
árbol devorado y humoso,
cerrazón de noche, carbón consumado,
enebro denso, ciprés engañoso,
cierto a los ojos, huido en la mano.

En una pura noche se hizo mi luto
en el dédalo de mi cuerpo
y me cubrió este resuello
noche y humo que llaman luto
que me envuelve y que me ciega.

Mourning

In one single night there burst from my breast
the tree of mourning; it heightened and grew,
pushed my bones, split my flesh,
till its crown reached my head.

It spread great leaves and branches
over my shoulder, over my back,
and in three days I was covered,
rich with it as with my blood.
Where can they touch me now?
What arm shall I give that is not of mourning?

Like billows of smoke
I am no longer flame or ember.
I am this spiral, this liana,
this wheeling of dense smoke.

Those who come to see me still
call me by name, see my face.
But I, who smother, see myself
a devoured and smoking tree,
pitch of night, consumed carbon,
thick juniper, a deluding cypress,
real to the eye, fled from the hand.

In one pure night my mourning shaped
in the labyrinth of my body,
and this night breath enveloped me,
this smoke they call mourning that
engulfs and blinds me.

Mi último árbol no está en la tierra
no es de semilla ni de leño,
no se plantó, no tiene riegos.
Soy yo misma mi ciprés
mi sombreadura y mi ruedo,
mi sudario sin costuras,
y mi sueño que camina
árbol de humo y con ojos abiertos.

En lo que dura una noche
cayó mi sol, se fué mi día,
y mi carne se hizo humareda
que corta un niño con la mano.

El color se escapó de mis ropas,
el blanco, el azul, se huyeron
y me encontré en la mañana
vuelta un pino de pavesas.

Ven andar un pino de humo,
me oyen hablar detrás de mi humo
y se cansarán de amarme,
de comer y de vivir,
bajo de triángulo oscuro
falaz y crucificado
que no cría más resinas
y raíces no tiene ni brotes.
Un solo color en las estaciones,
un solo costado de humo
y nunca un racimo de piñas
para hacer el fuego, la cena y la dicha.

My final tree is not of the earth,
not of seed, not of wood,
not planted, not watered.
I myself am my own cypress,
my obscure shade, my circumference,
my own unsewn cerement,
and my dream that walks,
a smoking tree with opened eyes.

In the space of one night
my sun fell, my day vanished.
My body became a cloud of smoke
that a child can cut with his hand.

The colors left my clothes;
the white, the blue fled,
and in the morning I found myself
a pine tree of burnt embers.

They see a smouldering pine that walks,
they hear me speak behind my smoke,
and they will grow weary of loving me,
of eating and living
beneath this dark triangle
fallacious and crucified
that bears no more resin,
has no roots, no new growth.
One single color through all the seasons,
one single flank of smoke
and never a cluster of pine cones
to make fire, supper, and joy.

Ayudadores

Mientras el niño se me duerme,
sin que lo sepa ni la tierra,
por ayudarme en acabarlo
sus cabellos hace la hierba,
sus deditos la palma-dátil
y las uñas la buena cera.
Los caracoles dan su oído
y la fresa roja su lengua,
y el arroyo le trae risas
y el monte le manda paciencias.

(Cosas dejé sin acabar
y estoy confusa y con vergüenza:
apenas sienes, apenas habla,
apenas bulto que le vean.)

Los que acarrean van y vienen,
entran y salen por la puerta
trayendo orejitas de *cuye*
y unos dientes de concha-perla.

Tres Navidades y será otro,
de los tobillos a la cabeza:
será talludo, será recto
como los pinos de la cuesta.

Y yo iré entonces voceándolo
como una loca por los pueblos,
con un pregón que van a oírme
las praderías y los cerros.

The Helpers

While my baby sleeps,
the earth, unaware,
helps me to finish him.
The grass makes his hair,
the date-palm his fingers,
and the beeswax his nails.
The seashells give him hearing,
the red strawberry his tongue,
the rivulet brings him smiles,
and the mountain sends him patience.

(I left my baby unfinished
and I am confused and ashamed:
scarcely a brow, scarcely a voice,
scarcely a size you can see.)

They carry things, go and come,
enter and leave the door,
bringing tiny chipmunk ears,
teeth of mother-of-pearl.

In three Christmases he will be another,
changed from head to toe.
Tall as a reed he will stand,
straight as the pine tree on the slope.

Then, like a crazy woman,
I will proclaim him through the town
with a shouting clearly heard
by the hills and meadows around.

Campeón Finlandés[1]

Campeón finlandés, estás tendido
en la relumbre de tu último Stadium,
rojo como el faisán en su vida y su muerte,
de heridas pespunteado y apurado
gárgola viva de tu propio sangre.

Has caído en las nieves de tu infancia,
en filos azulados y en espejos acérrimos
diciendo ¡no! hacia el Norte y el Este,
un ¡no! que aprieta los gajos de nieve,
endurece como diamantes los *skíes*
y para el tanque como un jabalí...
Nadador, pelotaris, corredor,
que te quemen el nombre y te llamen "Finlandia."
Benditos sean tu última pista,
el meridiano que tomó tu cuerpo
y el sol de medianoche, que te cedió el milagro.

Negaste al invasor el sorbo de tus lagos,
tus caminos y la hebra de tus renos,
el umbral de tu casa, el cubo de tu arena,
el arco-iris de las Vírgenes de Cristo,
la bautizada frente de tus niños.

[1] Durante la segunda guerra mundial, Finlandia ofreció increíble resistencia a dos invasiones rusas y, al pesar de grandes perdidas, mantuvo su autonomia.

Finnish Champion[1]

Finnish Champion, you are stretched out
in the burnished light of your final stadium,
red as the pheasant in life and in death,
stitched with wounds, drained as a gargoyle spout
of your own blood.

You have fallen in the snows of your childhood,
among blue edges and steely mirrors,
crying No! to the North and the East,
a No! that compresses profusion of snow,
hardens the skis to diamonds,
stops the war tank like a wild boar.
Swimmer, ball-player, runner,
let them burn your name and call you "Finland."
Hallowed be your final course,
hallowed the meridian that took your body,
hallowed the midnight sun that granted your final miracle.

You denied the invader the draught of your lakes,
your paths, the life-thread of your reindeer,
the threshold of your home, the cube of your arena,
the rainbow of your Virgins of Christ,
the baptized foreheads of your children.

[1] During World War II Finland put up amazing resistance to two massive invasions by Russian forces, and despite heavy losses succeeded in retaining her autonomy.

Te miran tus quinientos lagos
que probaron tu cuerpo uno por uno.
Se empina, atarantada, por saberte, la morsa,
como cuando gritabas la Maratón ganada,
y dos renos te echan el humo del aliento
en dos pitones blancos que se hacen y deshacen . . .

Para que no te aúllen, te bailen ni te befen
esta noche los tártaros dementes,
cuyas botas humean de nieve y tropelía,
las mujeres te conducimos como a un hijo,
alzamos la nonada de tu cuerpo
y vamos a quemarte en tus pinos del Norte.

No lloran ni las madres ni los niños,
ni aun el hielo, en la Finlandia enjuta
como la Macabea, que da sudor de sangre
y da de mamar sangre, pero no llora llanto;
y nosotras tampoco lloramos, atizando
el ruedo y los cogollos de tu hoguera.

La hoguera es alta como el trance, y arde
sin humo y sin ceniza, toda en fucsias y en dalias,
mientras suena el infierno de los tanques,
la frontera de su metal, castañetea
y caen los aviones en sesgo de vergüenza . . .

Five hundred Finnish lakes that, one by one,
tested your body, now turn their gaze on you.
The walrus heaves himself up to behold you,
wonder-struck as on that day of the Marathon
when you cried out your victory.
Reindeer blow on your fallen body their smokey breath
like two white snakes that form and vanish.

Lest mad Tartars this night
howl and dance over you, lest they mock you,
their boots smoking with snow and atrocity,
we women carry you like a son.
We raise the waste of your body
to burn it on a pyre of your pine trees.

Finnish mothers do not weep, nor Finnish children.
Not even ice weeps in Finland,
dry as the mother of Maccabaeus who sweat blood,
was milked of blood, but wept no tears.
We, too, do not weep, stirring
the wheel, the blazing heart's whorl of your fire.

The bonfire flares high,
smokeless, ashless, all fuscia and dahlia,
while the hell of war tanks resounds,
the frontier of metal rattles,
and planes fall twisting in shame ...

Campeón finlandés, saltas ahora
más hermoso que en todos tus Stadiums.
Subes y vas oreando tu sangre
con el rollo del viento que te enjuga.
¡Partes el cielo, ríes y lloras
al abrazar a Judas Macabeo!

Finnish Champion, you leap up now
more beautiful than in all your stadiums.
You rise, airing your blood
in the toss of winds that dry you.
You part the heavens with your laughter, your cry,
embracing Judas Maccabaeus!

El Regreso

Desnudos volvemos a nuestro Dueño,
manchados como el cordero
de matorrales, gredas, caminos,
y desnudos volvemos al abra
cuya luz nos muestra desnudos:
y la Patria del arribo
nos mira fija y asombrada.

Pero nunca fuimos soltados
del coro de las Potencias
y de las Dominaciones,
y nombre nunca tuvimos,
pues los nombres son del Unico.

Soñamos madres y hermanos,
rueda de noches y días
y jamás abandonamos
aquel día sin soslayo.
Creímos cantar, rendirnos
y después seguir el canto;
pero tan sólo ha existido
este himno sin relajo.

Y nunca fuimos soldados,
ni maestros ni aprendices,
pues vagamente supimos
que jugábamos al tiempo
siendo hijos de lo Eterno.

The Return

Naked we return to our Lord,
stained as sheep
with briar, marl, and dust of the road.
Naked we return to the haven
whose light uncovers us;
the kingdom of our arrival
stares in astonishment.

Yet we were never set loose
from the choir of powers,
the choir of dominions;
we never had a name
since all names are the One.

Mothers and brothers we dreamed,
dreamed the wheel of nights and days.
We never departed that
one unending day.
We only believed we sang
and grew weary
and later sang again.
But only one hymn is
eternally sung.

Never were we soldiers,
not master or apprentice.
We vaguely knew
we only played at time
as children of eternity.

Y nunca esta Patria dejamos,
y lo demás, sueños han sido,
juegos de niños en patio inmenso:
fiestas, luchas, amores, lutos.

Dormidos hicimos rutas
y a ninguna parte arribábamos,
y al Angel Guardián rendimos
con partidas y regresos.

Y los Angeles reían
nuestros dolores y nuestras dichas
y nuestras búsquedas y hallazgos
y nuestros pobres duelos y triunfos.

Caíamos y levantábamos,
cocida la cara de llanto,
y lo reído y lo llorado,
y las rutas y los senderos,
y las partidas y los regresos,
las hacían con nosotros,
el costado en el costado.

Y los oficios jadeados
nunca, nunca los aprendíamos:
el cantar, cuando era el canto,
en la garganta roto nacía.

No, we never left that kingdom;
all else has been but dreams,
games of children in a boundless patio,
playing, fighting, loving, grieving.

Out on journeys in our sleep
we arrived nowhere at all.
But our guardian angel was weary
of all the goings and comings.

Our grief and our joy,
our searches and discoveries,
our pain and triumph
made all the angels laugh.

We fell and got up,
faces crumpled with weeping,
with laughing and crying,
with roads and pathways,
departures and returns—
and in all these things
angels were at our side.

But we never learned, never,
hard-panting work.
Even singing, when we sang,
burst ragged from our throats.

De la jornada a la jornada
jugando a huerta, a ronda, o canto,
al oficio sin Maestro,
a la marcha sin camino,
y a los nombres sin las cosas
y a la partida sin arribo
fuimos niños, fuimos niños,
inconstantes y desvariados.

Y baldíos regresamos,
¡tan rendidos y sin logro!
balbuceando nombres de "patrias"
a las que nunca arribamos.

Playing at orchard, dance, or song,
playing at crafts without Master,
at walk without path,
at names without things,
at departures without arrivals,
from one day's journey to the next
we were children; we were
crazy inconstant children.

We returned, vagrant,
exhausted, nothing gained,
babbling the names of countries
we had never seen.

Ultimo Arbol

Esta solitaria greca
que me dieron en naciendo:
lo que va de mi costado
a mi costado de fuego;

lo que corre de mi frente
a mis pies calenturientos;
esta Isla de mi sangre,
esta parvedad de reino,

yo lo devuelvo cumplido
y en brazada se lo entrego
al último de mis árboles,
a tamarindo o a cedro.

Por si en la segunda vida
no me dan lo que ya dieron
y me hace falta este cuajo
de frescor y de silencio,

y yo paso por el mundo
en sueño, carrera o vuelo,
en vez de umbrales de casas,
quiero árbol de paradero.

Le dejaré lo que tuve
de ceniza y firmamento,
mi flanco lleno de hablas
y mi flanco de silencio;

Final Tree

This solitary fretwork
they gave me at birth
that goes from side
to fiery side,

that runs from my forehead
to my hot feet,
this island of my blood,
this minuteness of kingdom,

I return it fulfilled.
With arms outstretched I give it
to the last of my trees,
to tamarinth or cedar.

In case in the second life
they will not give again what has been given
and I should miss this solace
of freshness and silence,

and if I should pass through the world
in dream, running or flying,
instead of thresholds of houses
I shall want a tree to rest under.

I bequeath it all I had
of ash and firmament,
my flank of speech,
my flank of silence.

soledades que me dí,
soledades que me dieron,
y el diezmo que pagué al rayo
de mi Dios dulce y tremendo;

mi juego de toma y daca
con las nubes y los vientos,
y lo que supe, temblando,
de manantiales secretos.

¡Ay, arrimo tembloroso
de mi Arcángel verdadero,
adelantado en las rutas
con el ramo y el ungüento!

Tal vez ya nació y me falta
gracia de reconocerlo,
o sea el árbol sin nombre
que cargué como a hijo ciego.

A veces cae a mis hombros
una humedad o un oreo
y veo en contorno mío
el cíngulo de su ruedo.

Pero tal vez su follaje
ya va arropando mi sueño
y estoy, de muerta, cantando
debajo de él, sin saberlo.

Loneliness I gave myself,
loneliness they gave me,
the small tithe I paid the lightning
of my God, sweet and tremendous.

My play of give and take
with clouds and with the winds
and what I knew, trembling,
of secret springs.

Ay! Tremulous shelter
of my true Archangel,
ahead on every road
with branch and balsam.

Perhaps it is already born
and I lack the grace to know it,
or it was that nameless tree
I carried like a blind son.

At times a dampness falls
around my shoulders, a soft breeze,
and I see about me
the girdle of my tree.

Perhaps its foliage
already clothes my dream
and in death I sing beneath it
without knowing.

Ultimo Arbol

Pero tal vez su follaje
ya va arropando mi sueño

Final Tree

Perhaps its foliage
already clothes my dream

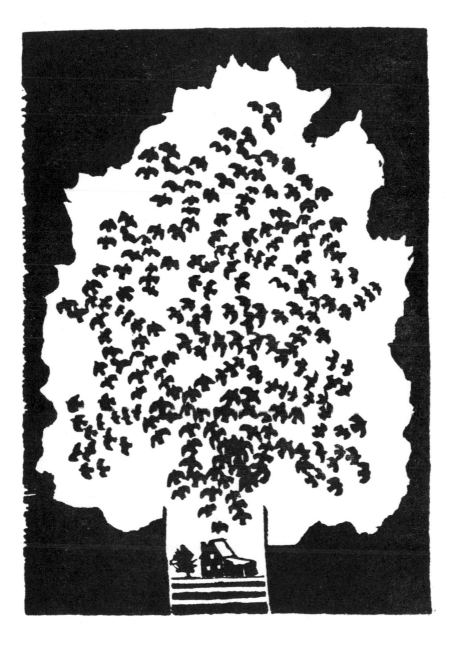

Index of Themes

Poems of Young Love and Sorrow

Tenderness: Poems for Mothers and Children

The Teacher and Poems for Teaching

THE JOHNS HOPKINS PRESS
Designed by Arlene J. Sheer
Composed in Granjon text and Garamont display
by Monotype Composition Company

Printed on 70 lb. Mohawk Vellum
by Vinmar Lithographing Company
Bound by L. H. Jenkins, Inc.